Summertime
Quilts

Summertime
Quilts
Fresh Designs in Chenille

Patti Eaton

Martingale®
& COMPANY

Credits

President ◆ Nancy J. Martin
CEO ◆ Daniel J. Martin
Publisher ◆ Jane Hamada
Editorial Director ◆ Mary V. Green
Managing Editor ◆ Tina Cook
Technical Editor ◆ Laurie Baker
Copy Editor ◆ Ellen Balstad
Design Director ◆ Stan Green
Illustrator ◆ Laurel Strand
Cover and Text Designer ◆ Shelly Garrison
Photographer ◆ Brent Kane

That Patchwork Place® is an imprint of Martingale & Company®.

Summertime Quilts: Fresh Designs in Chenille © 2005 by Patti Eaton

Martingale & Company
20205 144th Avenue NE
Woodinville, WA 98072-8478 USA
www.martingale-pub.com

Printed in China
10 09 08 07 06 05   8 7 6 5 4 3 2 1

Library of Congress Cataloging-in-Publication Data

Eaton, Patti.
    Summertime quilts : fresh designs in chenille / Patti Eaton.
        p. cm.
    ISBN 1-56477-579-8
    1. Quilting—Patterns. 2. Patchwork—Patterns. 3. Chenille. I. Title
    TT835.E29 2005
    746.46'041—dc22

                                        2004020684

Mission Statement
Dedicated to providing quality products and service to inspire creativity.

Acknowledgments

This is the second time I've gone through the process of getting a book together to submit to a publisher. Those of you who have done it know what it takes; for those of you who haven't, let me just say that I didn't do it all by myself. I would like to give special thanks to a few people who helped me make it all possible.

- My staff and supporters at my quilt shop, the Hawthorne Gallery, whom I affectionately refer to as "The Gallery Girls," for all of their extra help. They critiqued my designs, helped select fabrics, bound quilts, and just generally picked up after me as I scattered paper and pencils, cutters, rulers, scissors, and more along my path.

- Pat Owen, longtime friend and former staff member, for piecing "Summers on the Farm Quilt" and helping with all the other little details.

- Sandy Hawks, who juggles managing the store and teaching, as well as quilting most of the book projects. She does it all with humor and style.

- Lorrie Bensel, who just began her machine-quilting career and quilted "Summers on the Farm Quilt." I admire her creativity and enthusiasm.

- My very special friend, mentor, and coach, Pam Mostek. None of this would have been possible without her help. Thank you.

- My husband, Lester, who is never fazed by my ventures and who thinks that I can do it all. Your support and efforts have not gone unnoticed.

- My technical editor, Laurie Baker, and all the people at Martingale & Company. Thank you for all that you have done to make this book as good as it can be.

- Cranston Print Works, for generously supplying a good portion of the red fabrics that were used for "Maggie's 'Headboard'" and "Red Tulips Quilt," and Fabric Café for the Chenille by the Inch.

- And, of course, all of you quilters. Because of you I can do what I love— design quilts.

Contents

Introduction

So how is it, you may ask, that a busy shop owner who usually prefers traditional quilts can get sidetracked onto chenille? Well, to be completely honest, I am first and foremost a collector of stuff. My friends would say I collect too much stuff, but I always think that I am going to need or use the things for something and I usually do. Old chenille bedspreads are just one of my many collecting passions.

Chenille bedspreads used to be $5 to $10 at yard sales for really nice ones, and "cutters" (the ones with irreparable damage) were even less. Of course, I had to have them. I used them to make typical things like stuffed bunnies and bears, giving many away and selling some in my shop. My friend Pam and I would go to my basement sewing room and literally dig through bags of used chenille looking for the perfect pieces to use. When we both were cutting and sewing, the air would be full of the fluff stuff and we would, from time to time, have to come up for air. Fuzz would cling to our hair, our clothes, and our faces. We had loads of fun and never gave a thought to the possibility of diminishing supplies of old chenille spreads, but it happened. Nice, old chenille spreads are hard to come by these days, so when I discovered sources for new chenille, my shop just had to have that, too!

Customer reaction to chenille has been interesting to observe. The mature quilter almost always fondly remembers chenille from her past, like the bedspread on her grandmother's bed. My

younger shoppers are drawn to chenille as something new and cozy. So, what do they do with it? Well, they do what we do at Hawthorne Gallery—make quilts.

For this book, I wanted to design room settings that combine the two things I love best: traditional piecing and big pieces of pretty chenille. My machine quilter found that chenille responds well to loose, open quilting designs. But what was it that really lit my fire to use chenille? A granddaughter. Along came Naomi and I had to have a special place just for her. I decided on a large walk-in closet under the eaves, off the upstairs master bedroom in my 1913 cottage bungalow. It still has its original wallpaper, a white ground with pink butterflies and flowers, and the rose-colored carpet that someone had added before we bought the house. There's a small window about two feet off the floor that is just the right size for little eyes to view the

world. All in all, the room is perfect for Grandma Patti to let her imagination run wild, and believe me, I don't have a "less-is-more" attitude in this room. This room is totally girly, and I have used chenille, old and new, everywhere. In fact, there's so much chenille that we call Naomi's special spot Chenille Heaven.

It is my goal with this book to inspire others to experience the relaxing look chenille provides and to realize that once again, what's old is new. If you are fortunate enough to have vintage chenille, get it out and use it along with the new. Chenille is 100% cotton, which means that it is washable and durable. It comes in many colors and can even be overstitched for added design possibilities. It has stood the test of time, so isn't now the time for you to give it a try? Hopefully I have you thinking and planning to use just a little bit, or maybe a lot, of chenille to create a little bit of heaven at your house, too!

Tulips and Baskets Quilt

A cheery combination of Basket blocks and Tulip blocks gives a summertime feeling to this wonderful wall hanging or table topper. I selected sky blues and intense reds to convey the feeling of a fresh new day. You may choose to substitute fabrics in your favorite colors, keeping in mind that the background fabrics should contrast with your tulip and basket fabric choices.

Materials

Yardages are based on 42"-wide fabrics.

- ⅜ yard *each* of 4 different medium blues for Basket blocks
- ¾ yard *total* of at least 4 assorted reds for Tulip and Basket blocks
- ¾ yard *total* of at least 4 assorted creams for sashing
- ⅝ yard *total* of at least 4 assorted light to medium blues for Tulip blocks
- ¼ yard of green for Tulip blocks
- 1¼ yards of fabric for backing
- ½ yard of blue for binding
- 40" x 40" piece of batting

Cutting

All measurements include ¼"-wide seam allowances.

From *each* of the 4 medium blues for Basket blocks, cut:

1 square, 6⅞" x 6⅞"; cut each square in half once diagonally to yield 2 triangles. You will use 1 triangle and have 1 left over.

1 strip, 1½" x 42"; crosscut the strip into:

   1 rectangle, 1½" x 7"
   1 rectangle, 1½" x 6"
   1 rectangle, 1½" x 2½"
   1 square, 1½" x 1½"

From the assorted reds, cut a *total* of:

4 squares, 4⅞" x 4⅞"; cut each square in half once diagonally to yield 8 triangles. You will use 1 triangle from each square and have 1 left over.

12 squares, 2⅞" x 2⅞"*
16 squares, 2½" x 2½"*
108 squares, 1½" x 1½"

From the assorted creams, cut a *total* of:

72 rectangles, 1½" x 6½"
8 rectangles, 1½" x 5½"

From the assorted light to medium blues for Tulip blocks, cut a *total* of:

12 squares, 2⅞" x 2⅞"
12 rectangles, 1½" x 5½"
12 rectangles, 1½" x 4½"
36 rectangles, 1½" x 2½"
12 squares, 1½" x 1½"

From the green, cut:

4 strips, 1½" x 42"; crosscut the strips into:

   12 rectangles, 1½" x 5½"
   12 rectangles, 1½" x 4½"

From the binding fabric, cut:

4 strips, 2½" x 42"

In order for the tulip petals in each block to be the same, cut one 2½" square from the same fabric as you cut each 2⅞" square.

Making the Basket Blocks

When making these blocks, be sure to use the blue pieces you cut for the Basket blocks—not the Tulip blocks.

1. Sew a blue 1½" x 6" rectangle to one short side of each red triangle as shown on page 14. The end of the strip will extend beyond the long side of the triangle. Sew a matching blue

Finished quilt size: 34" x 34" ◆ Finished block size: 8"

1½" x 7" rectangle to the adjacent side of the red triangle as shown. Trim the excess ends flush with the base of the triangle.

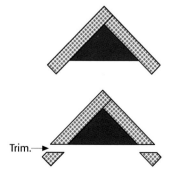

Trim.→

2. Sew each basket top unit from step 1 to a matching blue triangle basket base as shown. The unit should measure 6½" x 6½".

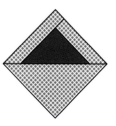

3. Sew a blue 1½" square to one end of four cream 1½" x 5½" rectangles. To the right edge of each basket base, position and sew one of these blue/cream units; make sure the

blues match. Sew a blue 1½" x 2½" rectangle to one end of each of the remaining cream 1½" x 5½" rectangles. To the left side of each basket base, position and sew one of the blue/cream units; make sure the blues match.

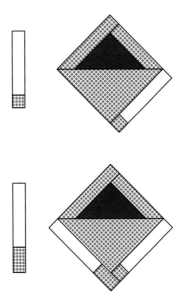

4. Sew a red 1½" square to one end of four cream 1½" x 6½" rectangles. Position and sew one of these units to the right edge of each basket handle. Sew a red 1½" square to both ends of four cream 1½" x 6½" rectangles. Position and sew one of these units to the left side of each basket handle.

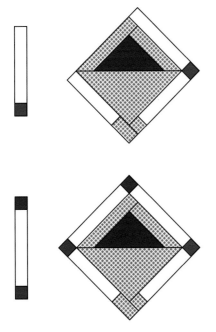

5. With a soft-leaded pencil, draw a diagonal line on the wrong side of four red 2½" squares. With right sides together, position a square on the bottom corner of each basket base as shown. Stitch on the drawn line. Flip the top half of the red square toward the bottom of the block and press it in place. Trim away the bottom two layers ¼" from the sewn line. Square up each block, if necessary, so that it measures 8½" x 8½".

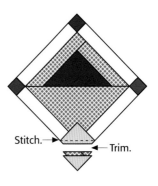

Stitch.→ ←Trim.

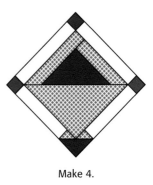

Make 4.

Making the Tulip Blocks

1. Sew a red 1½" square to one side of each blue 1½" square. Stitch a blue 1½" x 2½" rectangle to one long side of each pair as shown. Make 12 units. Each unit should measure 2½" square.

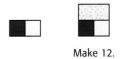

Make 12.

2. Pair each blue 2⅞" square with a red 2⅞" square, right sides together, with the blue squares on top. Draw a diagonal line from corner to corner on the wrong side of each blue

square. Stitch ¼" from each side of the drawn lines. Cut the squares apart on the drawn lines and press open the 24 resulting triangle squares.

Make 24.

3. Join one red 2½" square, two matching triangle squares from step 2 that use the same red fabric as the 2½" square, and one unit from step 1 into two rows as shown. Stitch the units in each row together, and then stitch the rows together. Make 12 units.

Make 12.

4. Sew a blue 1½" x 4½" rectangle to the bottom of each unit from step 3, and then sew a blue 1½" x 5½" rectangle to the left side of each unit as shown.

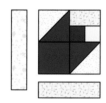

5. Place a blue 1½" x 2½" rectangle at one end of each green 1½" x 4½" rectangle as shown, right sides together. Draw a diagonal line on each blue rectangle that goes from the lower left corner to the upper edge where the two rectangles intersect. Sew on the drawn line,

and then trim ¼" from the stitching line. Press the blue rectangle up. The pieced rectangles should measure 1½" x 5½".

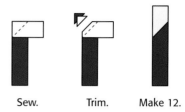

Sew.   Trim.   Make 12.

6. Place a blue 1½" x 2½" rectangle at one end of each green 1½" x 5½" rectangle as shown, right sides together. Draw a diagonal line on each blue rectangle that goes from the lower right corner to the upper edge where the two rectangles intersect. Sew on the drawn line, and then trim ¼" from the stitching line. Press the blue rectangle up. The pieced rectangles should measure 1½" x 6½".

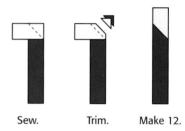

Sew.   Trim.   Make 12.

7. Stitch the pieced rectangles from step 5 to the bottom of the units from step 4 as shown. Stitch the pieced rectangles from step 6 to the left side of the units as shown.

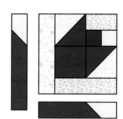 

8. Sew a cream 1½" x 6½" rectangle to the right and left sides of each unit from step 7 as shown. Sew a red 1½" square to each end of the remaining cream 1½" x 6½" rectangles. Stitch one of these pieced rectangles to the

top and bottom of each unit as shown. Set the remaining pieced rectangles aside for the outer border. Square up each block, if necessary, so that it measures 8½" x 8½".

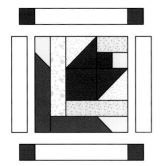

Make 12.

Assembling the Quilt Top

1. Arrange the Basket blocks and Tulip blocks into four horizontal rows as shown. Sew the blocks in each row together. Press the seams in opposite directions from row to row. Stitch the rows together. Press the seams in one direction.

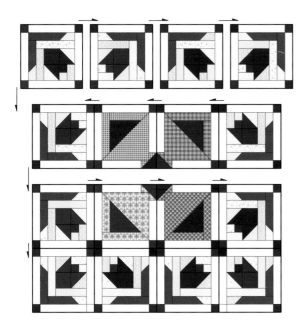

2. Join four of the units you set aside in step 8 of "Making the Tulip Blocks" end to end to make one long strip. Make four border strips.

Make 4.

3. Stitch a border strip to the sides of the quilt top. Stitch a red 1½" square to both ends of the remaining border strips. Stitch these strips to the top and bottom edges of the quilt top.

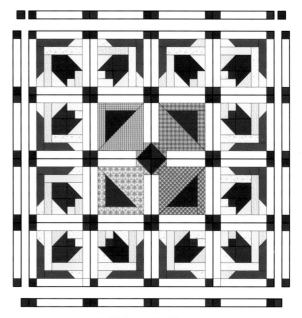

Quilt Assembly Diagram

Finishing the Quilt

1. Layer the quilt top with batting and backing; baste (refer to "Layering the Quilt" on page 90).

2. Hand or machine quilt as desired (refer to "Quilting" on page 91).

3. Add a hanging sleeve, if desired (refer to "Adding a Hanging Sleeve" on page 91).

4. Bind the quilt edges (refer to "Binding" on page 91).

Join the Parade Quilt

Like the colors of a Fourth of July parade, this happy quilt makes you smile and feel good all over. This quilt is all about enjoying the process of mixing cottons with chenille and adding embellishments.

Materials

Yardages are based on 42"-wide fabrics.

- 2 yards of red chenille for outer border
- 1½ yards *total* of assorted blues for Large Pinwheel blocks, Small Pinwheel blocks, and plain squares
- 1½ yards *total* of assorted reds for Large Pinwheel blocks, Small Pinwheel blocks, plain squares, and Tulip blocks
- 1 yard *total* of assorted chenille pieces for plain squares and rectangles
- 1 yard *total* of assorted creams for blocks
- 1 yard *total* of assorted yellows for Large Pinwheel blocks, Small Pinwheel blocks, plain squares, and Tulip blocks
- ½ yard or 1 fat quarter *each* of 2 different blues for Basket blocks
- ½ yard of multicolored stripe for inner border
- 1 fat quarter *each* of 2 floral prints for Basket blocks
- ¼ yard *total* of assorted greens for Tulip blocks
- 5 yards of fabric for backing
- ¾ yard of red for binding
- 80" x 88" piece of batting
- 1 package *each* of blue, white, light yellow, dark yellow, green, and red Chenille by the Inch (see "Embellishing with Faux Chenille" on page 86)

Cutting

All measurements include ¼"-wide seam allowances.

From *each* of the 2 different blues for Basket blocks, cut:

1 square, 12⅞" x 12⅞"; cut the square in half once diagonally to yield 2 triangles. You will use 1 triangle and have 1 left over.

1 rectangle, 2½" x 13"

1 rectangle, 2½" x 11"

1 rectangle, 2½" x 4½"

1 square, 2½" x 2½"

From *each* of the floral prints, cut:

1 square, 8⅞" x 8⅞"; cut each square in half once diagonally to yield 2 triangles. You will use 1 triangle and have 1 triangle left over.

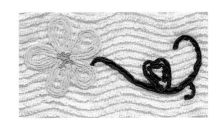

19

Finished quilt size: 75" x 83" ◆ Finished Basket block size: 16"
Finished size for plain squares, Large Pinwheel blocks, Tulip blocks, and Small Pinwheel blocks: 8"
Finished size for rectangles: 8" x 16"

From the assorted creams, cut a *total* of:

5 squares, 8⅞" x 8⅞"

1 rectangle, 8½" x 16½"

5 squares, 8½" x 8½"

4 squares, 4⅞" x 4⅞"*

2 squares, 4½" x 4½"

7 squares, 3⅜" x 3⅜"

4 rectangles, 2½" x 10½"

2 rectangles, 2½" x 14½"

2 rectangles, 2½" x 16½"

14 rectangles, 2½" x 3½"

7 rectangles, 1¾" x 3"

7 squares, 1¾" x 1¾"

7 rectangles, 1½" x 6½"

7 rectangles, 1½" x 5½"

From the assorted yellows, cut a *total* of:

3 squares, 8⅞" x 8⅞"

1 square, 8½" x 8½"

4 squares, 4⅞" x 4⅞"*

7 squares, 1¾" x 1¾"

From the assorted reds, cut a *total* of:

6 squares, 8⅞" x 8⅞"

3 squares, 8½" x 8½"

6 squares, 4⅞" x 4⅞"*

7 squares, 3⅜" x 3⅜"**

7 squares, 3" x 3"**

From the assorted greens, cut a *total* of:

7 rectangles, 2½" x 7½"

7 rectangles, 2½" x 5½"

From the assorted blues, cut a *total* of:

2 squares, 8⅞" x 8⅞"

2 squares, 8½" x 8½"

6 squares, 4⅞" x 4⅞"*

From the assorted chenille pieces, cut a *total* of:

3 rectangles, 8½" x 16½"

3 squares, 8½" x 8½"

From the multicolored stripe, cut:

7 strips, 2" x 42"

From the red chenille, cut:

8 strips, 8½" x 42"

From the binding fabric, cut:

9 strips, 2½" x 42"

* Cut these squares in pairs.

** In order for the tulip petals in each block to be the same, cut one 3" square from the same fabric as you cut each 3⅜" square.

Making the Basket Blocks

When making each block, select blue pieces that are cut from the same fabric.

1. Sew a blue 2½" x 11" rectangle to one short side of a floral triangle as shown. The end of the strip will extend beyond the long side of the triangle. Sew a blue 2½" x 13" rectangle to the adjacent side of the triangle as shown. Trim the excess ends flush with the long side of the triangle.

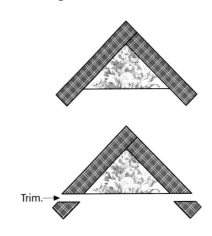

Trim.→

2. Sew the basket top unit from step 1 to a blue triangle basket base as shown. The unit should measure 12½" x 12½".

4. Sew a cream 2½" x 14½" rectangle to the right side of the handle. Sew a cream 2½" x 16½" rectangle to the left side of the handle.

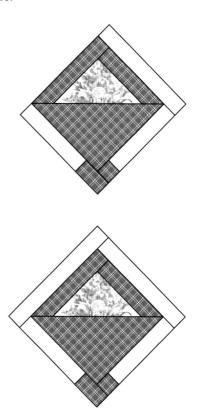

3. Sew a blue 2½" square to one end of a cream 2½" x 10½" rectangle. Position and sew the unit to the right edge of the basket base. Sew a blue 2½" x 4½" rectangle to one end of a cream 2½" x 10½" rectangle. Position and sew the unit to the left side of the basket base.

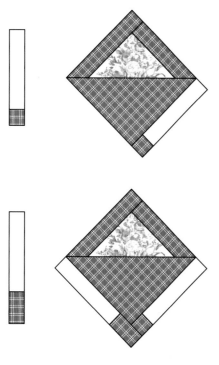

5. With a soft-leaded pencil, draw a diagonal line on the wrong side of a cream 4½" square. With right sides together, position the square on the bottom corner of the basket base as shown on the following page. Stitch on the drawn line. Flip the top half of the cream square toward the bottom of the block and

press it in place. Trim away the bottom two layers ¼" from the sewn line. Square up the block, if necessary, so that it measures 16½" x 16½".

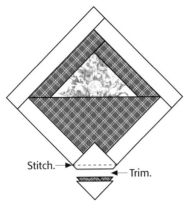

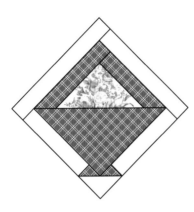

6. Repeat steps 1–5 to make one additional Basket block by using the pieces from the different blue print.

Making the Tulip Blocks

1. Sew a yellow 1¾" square to one side of each cream 1¾" square. Stitch a cream 1¾" x 3" rectangle to one long side of each pair as shown. Make seven. Each unit should measure 3" square.

Make 7.

2. Pair each cream 3⅜" square with a red 3⅜" square, right sides together, with the cream square on top. Draw a diagonal line from corner to corner on the wrong side of each cream square. Stitch ¼" from each side of the drawn lines. Cut the squares apart on the drawn lines and press open the 14 resulting triangle squares.

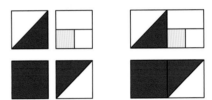

Make 14.

3. Join one red 3" square, two matching triangle squares from step 2 that use the same red fabric as the 3" square, and one unit from step 1 into two rows as shown. Stitch the units in each row together, and then stitch the rows together. Make seven units.

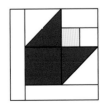

Make 7.

4. Sew a cream 1½" x 5½" rectangle to the bottom of each unit from step 3, and then sew a cream 1½" x 6½" rectangle to the left side of each unit as shown.

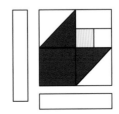

5. Place a cream 2½" x 3½" rectangle at one end of each green 2½" x 5½" rectangle as shown, right sides together. Draw a diagonal line on each cream rectangle that goes from the lower left corner to the upper edge where the two rectangles intersect. Sew on the drawn line, and then trim ¼" from the stitching line. Press the cream rectangle up. The pieced rectangles should measure 2½" x 6½".

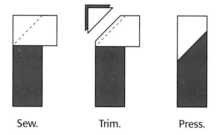

Sew.   Trim.   Press.

6. Place a cream 2½" x 3½" rectangle at one end of each green 2½" x 7½" rectangle as shown, right sides together. Draw a diagonal line on each cream rectangle that goes from the lower right corner to the upper edge where the two rectangles intersect. Sew on the drawn line, and then trim ¼" from the stitching line. Press the cream rectangle up. The pieced rectangles should measure 2½" x 8½".

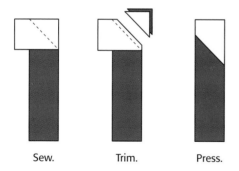

Sew.   Trim.   Press.

7. Stitch the pieced rectangles from step 5 to the bottom of the units from step 4 as shown. Stitch the pieced rectangles from step 6 to the left side of the units as shown.

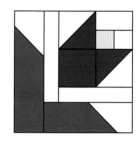

Make 7.

Making the Triangle Squares for the Large Pinwheel Blocks

1. Pair each of the three yellow 8⅞" squares with a red 8⅞" square, right sides together, with the yellow squares on top. Draw a diagonal line from corner to corner on the wrong side of each yellow square. Stitch ¼" from each side of the drawn lines. Cut the squares apart on the drawn lines and press open the six resulting triangle squares. You will use five triangle squares and have one left over.

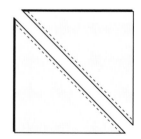

Make 6 (discard 1).

24

2. Repeat step 1 with three red and three cream 8⅞" squares to make six red-and-cream triangle squares. You will use five and have one left over. Make four blue-and-cream triangle squares by using two blue and two cream 8⅞" squares.

 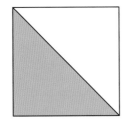

Make 6 (discard 1).   Make 4.

Making the Small Pinwheel Blocks

1. Pair each of two matching yellow 4⅞" squares with matching blue 4⅞" squares, right sides together, with the yellow squares on top. Repeat with the remaining yellow and two more blue 4⅞" squares. Pair two matching red 4⅞" squares with matching cream 4⅞" squares, right sides together, with the cream squares on top. Repeat with two more matching red 4⅞" squares and the remaining cream 4⅞" squares. Pair the remaining red 4⅞" squares with the remaining blue 4⅞" squares, right sides together, with the blue squares on top. Draw a diagonal line from corner to corner on the wrong side of each top square. Stitch ¼" from each side of the drawn lines. Cut the squares apart on the drawn lines and press open the resulting triangle squares.

Make 8.   Make 8.   Make 4.

2. Arrange four matching triangle squares into two rows, orienting the squares as shown. Stitch the squares in each row together, and then stitch the rows together. Make a total of five Small Pinwheel blocks.

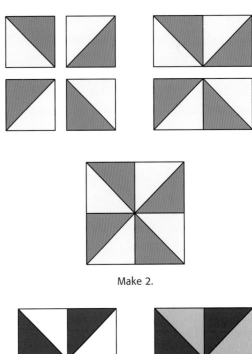

Make 2.

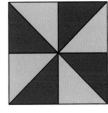

Make 2.   Make 1.

Assembling the Quilt Top

1. Refer to the quilt assembly diagram on page 26 to arrange the Basket blocks, Tulip blocks, triangle squares, Small Pinwheel blocks, 8½" plain squares and 8½" x 16½" rectangles as shown.

2. Follow the manufacturer's instructions and "Embellishing with Faux Chenille" on page 86 to transfer the designs on page 27 to the Basket blocks and rectangles. Decide if you would like any other blocks embellished and mark them with the desired design, referring to the photo on page 20 if necessary. Apply the chenille to the blocks.

3. Separate the blocks into groups as shown. Stitch the blocks in each group together. Sew the groups into two halves, and then stitch the halves together. Press the seams in each group in one direction, alternating the direction from group to group.

4. Refer to "Adding Borders" on page 87 to measure the quilt top for straight-cut borders. Piece the multicolored stripe 2" x 42" strips together and cut two strips the length needed for the side borders. Stitch the borders to the sides of the quilt top. Measure the quilt top for the top and bottom borders. Cut two strips the length needed and stitch the strips to the top and bottom edges of the quilt top. Repeat with the red chenille 8½" x 42" strips for the outer border.

Quilt Assembly Diagram

Finishing the Quilt

1. Layer the quilt top with batting and backing; baste (refer to "Layering the Quilt" on page 90).

2. Hand or machine quilt as desired (refer to "Quilting" on page 91).

3. Add a hanging sleeve, if desired (refer to "Adding a Hanging Sleeve" on page 91).

4. Bind the quilt edges (refer to "Binding" on page 91).

Chenille Patterns
Enlarge patterns 200%.

Basket Block Flower Pattern

Rectangle Block Flower Pattern

Basket Quilt

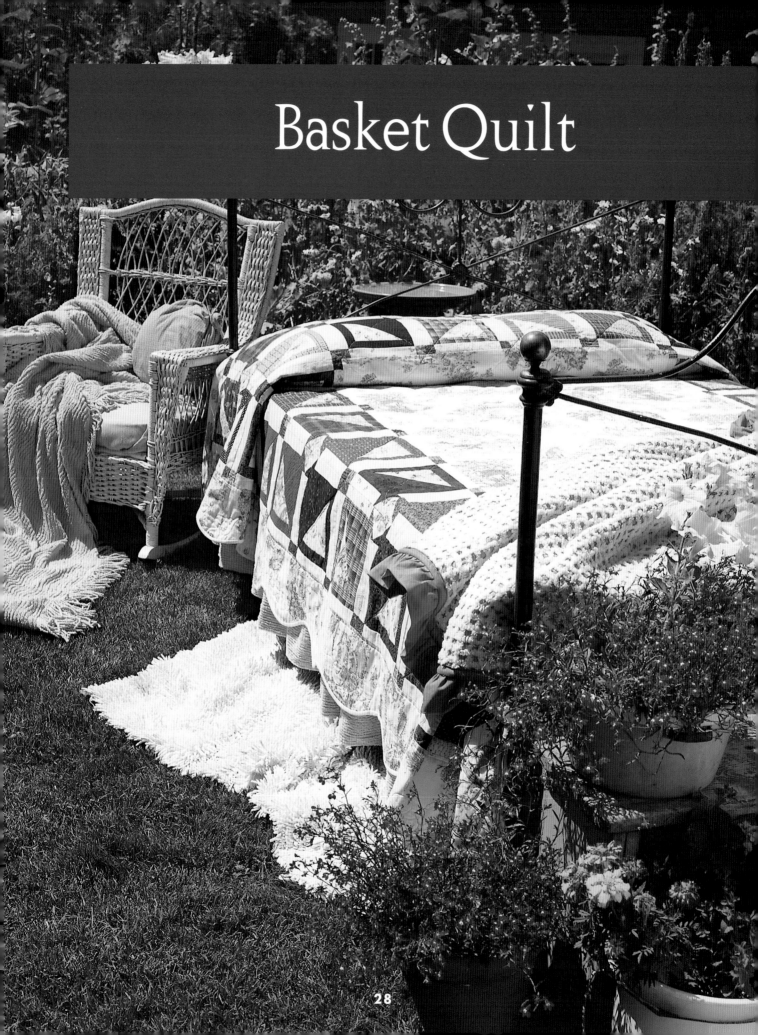

This design is perfect for a toile or other large-scale directional print. The blue-and-white color combination creates a cool and calm atmosphere that's just right for warm summer days. Furnish your bedroom with simple cottage furniture, which is often painted white, and accent with the bright colors of garden flowers to give your room loads of charm.

Materials

Yardages are based on 42"-wide fabrics.

- 5⅜ yards of blue-and-white toile for center panel and border*
- 3½ yards *total* of assorted light blue florals for blocks
- 28 rectangles, no smaller than 10" x 20", of assorted dark blue prints for blocks
- 7¾ yards of fabric for backing
- 1½ yards of fabric for binding
- 90" x 105" piece of batting
- Freezer paper
- Water-soluble marker

Yardage assumes the toile pattern runs the lengthwise grain of the fabric.

Cutting

All measurements include ¼"-wide seam allowances.

From the assorted dark blue prints, cut a total of:

15 strips, 1½" x 20"

From the remainder of one of the assorted dark blue prints, cut:

1 square, 7⅞" x 7⅞"; cut the square in half once diagonally to yield 2 triangles

2 rectangles, 1½" x 7"

2 rectangles, 1½" x 8"

2 rectangles, 1½" x 2½"

2 squares, 1½" x 1½"

(Makes 2 baskets. Repeat cutting instructions 28 times.)

From the assorted light blue florals, cut:

28 squares, 5⅞" x 5⅞"; cut each square in half once diagonally to yield 56 triangles

5 strips, 7½" x 42"; crosscut the strips into 10 strips, 7½" x 20"

5 strips, 6½" x 42"; crosscut the strips into 112 rectangles, 1½" x 6½"

4 strips, 2½" x 42"; crosscut the strips into 56 squares, 2½" x 2½"

From the blue-and-white toile, cut:

1 rectangle, 36½" x 54½", from the lengthwise grain

2 strips, 7½" x 101", from the lengthwise grain

3 strips, 7½" x 42", from the crosswise grain

3 strips, 2½" x 42", from the crosswise grain

Making the Basket Blocks

1. Sew a dark blue 1½" x 20" strip to a long edge of a light blue floral 7½" x 20" strip to make a strip set. Make five strip sets. Press the seam allowances toward the floral strips. Crosscut the strip sets into 56 segments, 1½" wide.

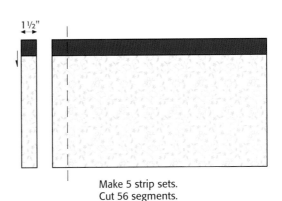

Make 5 strip sets.
Cut 56 segments.

Finished quilt size: 84" x 98"   ◆   Finished block size: 9"

2. Sew a dark blue 1½" x 20" strip to both long edges of a light blue floral 7½" x 20" strip. Make five strip sets. Press the seam allowances toward the floral strips. Crosscut the strip sets into 56 segments, 1½" wide.

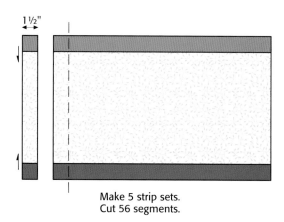

1½"

Make 5 strip sets.
Cut 56 segments.

3. Sew a dark blue 1½" x 7" rectangle to a short side of each light blue floral triangle as shown. The end of the strip will extend beyond the long side of the triangles. Sew a matching dark blue 1½" x 8" rectangle to the adjacent side of each triangle as shown. Trim the ends flush with the long side of the triangles.

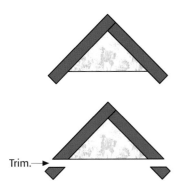

4. Sew each basket top unit from step 3 to a matching dark blue triangle basket base as shown. The units should measure 7½" x 7½".

5. Sew each dark blue 1½" square to one end of a light blue floral 1½" x 6½" rectangle. Position and sew a unit to the right edge of each basket base; make sure the dark blues match. Sew a dark blue 1½" x 2½" rectangle to one end of each of the remaining light

blue floral 1½" x 6½" rectangles. Position and sew a unit to the left side of each basket base; make sure the dark blues match.

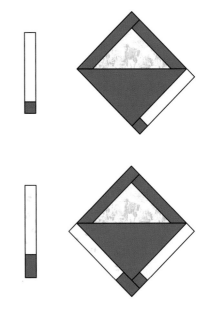

6. Stitch a segment from step 1 to the left side of each basket handle. Stitch a segment from step 2 to the right side of each basket handle.

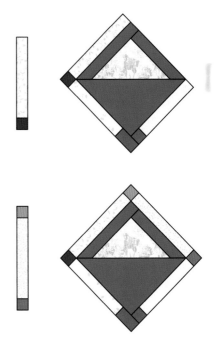

7. With a soft-leaded pencil, draw a diagonal line on the wrong side of each light blue floral 2½" square. With right sides together,

position the square on the bottom corner of the basket base as shown. Stitch on the drawn line. Flip the top half of the light blue square toward the bottom of the block and press it in place. Trim away the bottom two layers ¼" from the sewn line. Square up each block, if necessary, to 9½" x 9½".

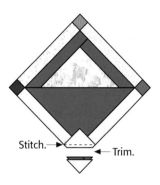

Make 56.

Assembling the Quilt Top

1. Sew six blocks into a row as shown for the sides of the quilt top. Make four rows. Press the seams in one direction. Sew eight blocks into a row as shown for the top and bottom of the quilt top. Make four rows. Press the seams in one direction.

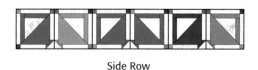

Side Row
Make 4.

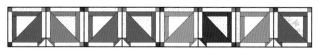

Top/Bottom Row
Make 4.

2. Stitch two side rows together as shown. Repeat for the remaining two rows. Stitch the joined rows to the sides of the toile 36½" x 54½" rectangle. Repeat to join the top/bottom block rows together as shown and stitch them to the top and bottom edges of the toile rectangle.

3. Align one end of a toile 7½" x 101" strip with the top edge of the quilt top, leaving the excess extending beyond the bottom edge of the quilt top as shown. Beginning at the upper edge, stitch the strip to the side of the quilt top, ending ¼" from the bottom edge. Repeat with the remaining side.

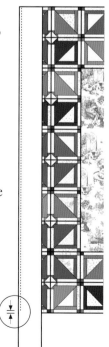

End stitching ¼" from bottom edge.

4. Stitch the three toile 7½" x 42" strips together end to end to make one long strip. From this strip, cut one 7½" x 90" bottom border strip and stitch it to the bottom edge of the quilt top, beginning and ending stitching ¼" from the corners.

5. Refer to "Mitered Borders" on page 88 to miter the corners at the bottom of the quilt top.

6. Sew the three toile 2½" x 42" strips together end to end to make one long strip. Measure the width of the quilt top through the center

and cut the strip to this measurement. Stitch the strip to the top edge of the quilt top.

Quilt Assembly Diagram

7. Refer to "Scalloped Edges" on page 89 to mark the scallops on the side and bottom edges of the border strips.

Finishing the Quilt

1. Layer the quilt top with batting and backing; baste (refer to "Layering the Quilt" on page 90).

2. Hand or machine quilt as desired (refer to "Quilting" on page 91).

3. Refer to "Bias Binding" on page 92 to cut and join enough 2½"-wide bias strips from the binding fabric to measure approximately 450". Trim the scallops on the marked lines and bind the quilt edges.

Chenille Bed Skirt

Finished bed skirt size: Full

Make this quick and easy chenille bed skirt as a complement to "Basket Quilt" on page 28 for an authentic cottage look. Standard bed skirts measure 14" from the top of the box spring to just above the floor, but because I designed this bed skirt to be used on a vintage iron bed that sits higher off the ground, the instructions are for a longer bed skirt with split corners that allow for the foot rails. Adjust the length of the drop according to your own needs. The skirt is attached to a large center piece or "deck" that lies between the box spring and mattress.

Materials

- ◆ 5½ yards of 45"-wide blue chenille for skirt panels
- ◆ 2½ yards of 60"-wide ticking for deck (large center piece)
- ◆ 10 yards of thin, strong cord or crochet thread

Cutting

All measurements include ¼"-wide seam allowances.

From the ticking, cut:

1 rectangle, 56½" x 77½"

From the blue chenille, cut:

2 strips, 21" x 113", from the lengthwise grain with a long edge along the selvage

1 strip, 21" x 81", from the lengthwise grain with a long edge along the selvage

> Use the leftover chenille to make "Star Pillow" on page 70.

Making the Bed Skirt

1. Turn under all of the raw edges of the 56½" x 77½" deck rectangle ½" and zigzag stitch them in place.

2. Zigzag stitch along the two short edges and one long raw edge of each of the three chenille skirt panels. The selvage edge of each panel will be gathered.

3. With the right side of each skirt panel face up, turn up the long edge opposite the selvage 5". Stitch ½" from each end of the hem allowance.

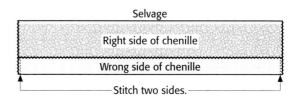

Selvage

Right side of chenille

Wrong side of chenille

Stitch two sides.

4. Turn the hem allowance on each panel so that it is wrong sides together. Turn the short unhemmed edges under ½" and stitch them in place, stitching from the selvage edge to the hem allowance as shown.

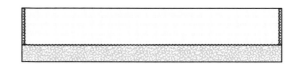

5. To gather each section, cut a length of cord or crochet thread several inches longer than the longest side of each skirt panel. Set your sewing machine for a wide zigzag stitch. With the excess cord extending beyond each end, place the cord ⅜" from the selvage edge of each panel and zigzag over it, being careful not to catch the cord in the stitching.

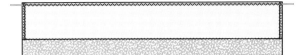

6. Mark the center point of each long side and a short end of the deck rectangle. Mark the center point of each skirt panel along the selvage edge. With the right sides up and the edges overlapping 1", pin the two side panels to the deck rectangle at the centers and ends. Pull on the cord ends to adjust the gathers to fit. Evenly distribute the gathers and pin the panels in place. Straight stitch just under the cord, and then remove the cord. Repeat with the end panel, overlapping the ends with the ends of the side panels.

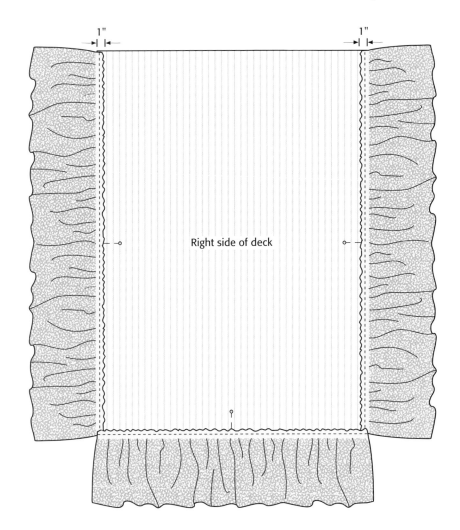

Right side of deck

Pillow Shams

Finished pillow sham size: 37" x 30"

Surround yourself with the comfort of blue-and-white pillow shams that offer a crisp, clean, and classic look. Not only do they work well with "Basket Quilt" (page 28) and "Chenille Duvet Cover" (page 40), they also would be wonderful tossed onto a porch swing or your favorite deck chair.

Materials

Yardages are based on 42"-wide fabrics. Materials given are enough for two pillow shams.

- 1¼ yards of blue-and-white toile for center
- ½ yard *total* of assorted whites for inner border
- ¼ yard *total* of assorted blues for inner border
- 4¾ yards of blue plaid for outer border and backing
- 1¾ yards of muslin for sham-top back
- 1 yard of blue print for binding
- 25" x 64" piece of thin batting
- Water-soluble marker

Cutting

All measurements include ¼"-wide seam allowances.

From the assorted blues, cut a *total* of:
   64 squares, 1½" x 1½"

From the assorted whites, cut a *total* of:
   28 rectangles, 1½" x 5½"

From the blue toile, cut:
   2 rectangles, 21½" x 28½"

From the blue plaid, cut:
   4 rectangles, 31" x 40"
   8 strips, 5½" x 40"

From the muslin, cut:
   2 rectangles, 36" x 43"

From the batting, cut:
   2 rectangles, 25" x 32"

Making the Pillow Sham Tops

1. Sew a blue 1½" square to both ends of each white 1½" x 5½" rectangle.

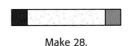

Make 28.

2. Sew three units from step 1 together end to end to make an inner side border strip. Make four inner side border strips. Stitch a side border strip to the short sides of each toile rectangle. Sew four units from step 1 together end to end. Then stitch a blue 1½" square to each end of each pieced strip. Make four inner top/bottom border strips. Stitch a border strip to the top and bottom edges of each toile rectangle.

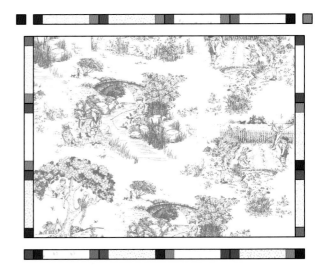

3. Refer to "Mitered Borders" on page 88 to add the blue plaid 5½" x 40" outer-border strips to the sides and then the top and bottom edges of each pillow sham top. Miter the corners.

4. Lay each muslin rectangle on a flat surface. Center a batting rectangle over each muslin rectangle. Center a pillow sham top over each batting rectangle, right side up. Refer to "Layering the Quilt" on page 90 to baste the layers together. Machine quilt the toile center as desired. Trim the batting so that it does not extend into the borders.

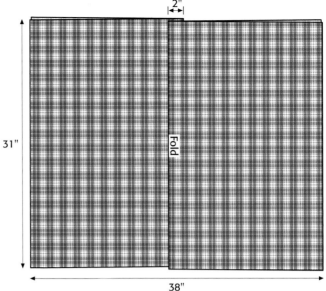

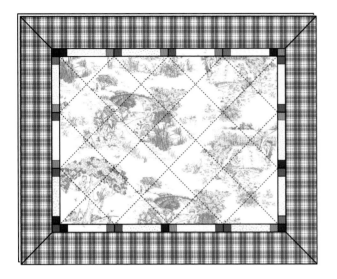

5. Refer to "Scalloped Edges" on page 89 to mark the scallops on the outer-border strips of each pillow sham top.

Finishing the Pillow Shams

1. Fold each blue plaid 31" x 40" rectangle in half to form a 31" x 20" rectangle; press the folded edge.

2. Overlap the folded edges of two rectangles 2" to create a 31" x 38" backing piece. Pin the pieces together along the folded edges. Repeat with the remaining two rectangles.

3. Center each pillow sham top, right side up, over a backing piece. Stitch on the scallop lines of each top. Stitch in the ditch of the inner border, following the inner and outer seam lines. Quilt a simple design in the outer border.

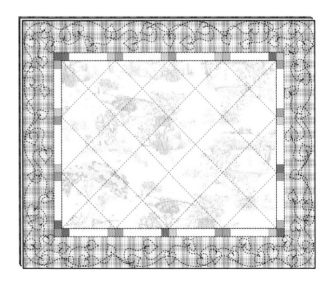

4. Refer to "Bias Binding" on page 92 to cut and join enough 2¼"-wide bias strips from the binding fabric to measure approximately 300". Trim the scallops on the marked lines and bind the pillow sham edges.

Chenille Duvet Cover

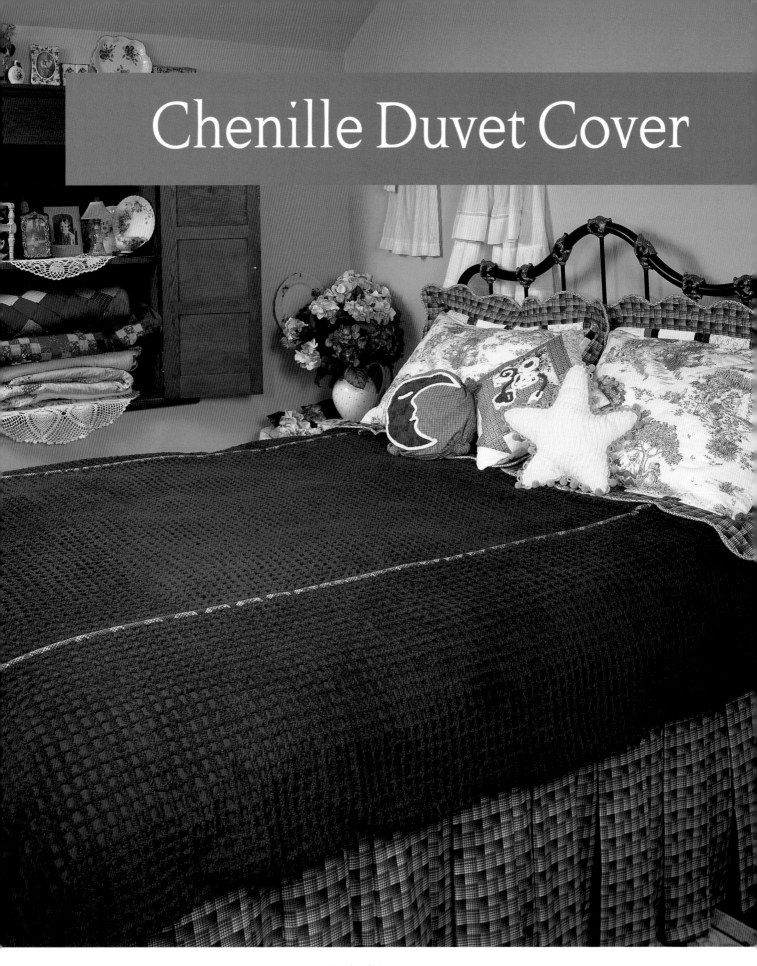

Finished size: Queen

As summer heats up, give your bedroom lots of visual impact with this cool, blue chenille duvet cover.

Backed with a blue-and-white toile, paired with the plaid bed skirt (page 46), and surrounded by pillows in

the same calm shades (page 37), it makes for lots of cottage-style charm.

Materials

Yardages are based on 42"-wide fabrics unless otherwise specified.

◆ 7 yards of 45"-wide blue chenille for cover top

◆ 1½ yards of blue plaid for bias trim

◆ 3⅝ yards of 108"-wide blue-and-white toile for backing*

◆ 7 yards of ⅜"-diameter cotton cording

◆ 10" dinner plate

◆ 8" salad plate

◆ 14 plastic 1"-diameter curtain rings

* If you use a 42"-wide toile, purchase 10½ yards.

Cutting

From the blue chenille, cut:

2 rectangles, 45" x 97"; crosscut 1 rectangle into 2 rectangles, 22½" x 97"

2 rectangles, 27" x 45"; crosscut 1 rectangle into 2 rectangles, 22½" x 27"

From the blue-and-white toile, cut:

1 strip, 3" x 108"; crosscut the strip into:

    5 strips, 3" x 4"

    5 strips, 3" x 12"

1 rectangle, 88" x 102"

1 rectangle, 27" x 88"

Making the Duvet Cover

1. Refer to "Bias Binding" on page 92 to cut and join enough 2"-wide bias strips from the blue plaid to measure approximately 252". Also from the blue plaid, cut and join enough 3½"-wide bias strips to measure 90". Set the 3½"-wide bias strip aside. Follow the instructions under "Making Custom Piping" on page 86 to cover the cotton cording with the 2"-wide bias strip.

2. With the raw edges aligned, pin the covered cording to one long edge of each chenille 22½" x 97" rectangle; stitch along the previous line of stitching with a zipper foot. Remove several stitches at both ends of the cording. Pull about 2" of the cording out of the casing at both ends and trim it off.

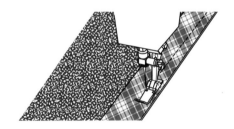

3. Pin a corded rectangle to each side of the chenille 45" x 97" rectangle, right sides together, with the corded rectangles on top. With a zipper foot, stitch inside the previous stitching line close to the cording.

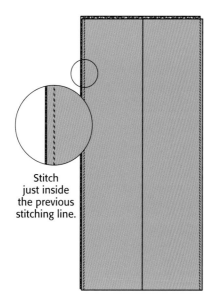

Stitch
just inside
the previous
stitching line.

Custom piping adds a professional touch.

4. Fold each of the toile 3" x 4" strips in half, right sides together, and stitch ¼" from the long edge. Turn the tubes to the right side. Position the seam so that it is in the center of the tube; press. Fold each tube in half

lengthwise with the seam to the inside. Thread two plastic rings onto each strip, and then fold each piece in half crosswise to make a loop.

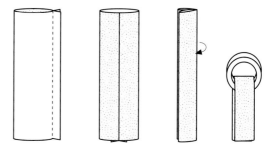

5. Pin the loops to the wrong side of the duvet top along the upper edge. Position one loop 3" from each end. Position the remaining loops 20" apart between the end loops.

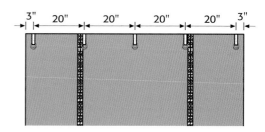

6. Place the right side of the plaid 3½"-wide bias strip on the wrong side of the duvet-top top edge, leaving ½" of strip extended beyond the ends of the top; stitch, securing the loops in the seam.

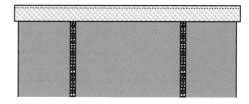

7. Press under the unstitched raw edge and ends of the bias strip ½", turning the ends over the raw edge of the chenille. Turn the long pressed edge to the front of the duvet top and topstitch

it in place along the pressed-under edges. For added strength, stitch through the base of the loops near the seam.

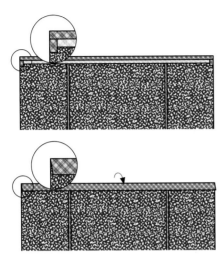

8. Lay your duvet top on a smooth, flat surface and gently round the bottom corners; use the 10" dinner plate as a guide. In the same manner, lay out the backing 88" x 102" rectangle and round the bottom corners; use the 8" salad plate as a guide.

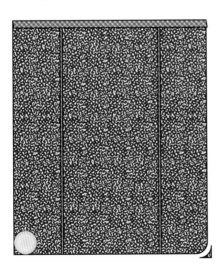

9. Fold the duvet top and backing piece in half lengthwise and mark the lengthwise center of each. With right sides together and centers aligned, place the backing over the top, positioning the bottom of the backing 2" above the bottom of the top. The backing will be narrower and longer than the top. The excess

around the edges is so that the top will wrap around to the back of the duvet and the backing will not show from the front. The excess at the top will be used to attach the pillow cover. Beginning at the bottom center, lift up the bottom edge of the backing piece and bring the bottom edge of the top to meet it, raw edges aligned. Pin the bottom and side edges together, up to but not over the plaid strip. Work in both directions and ease the fabric around the corners. There is a lot of fabric to deal with at this point, so go slowly and work carefully. An extra pair of hands is very helpful to take the cover to the machine. Stitch the bottom and sides with a scant ½" seam allowance. Turn the cover right side out.

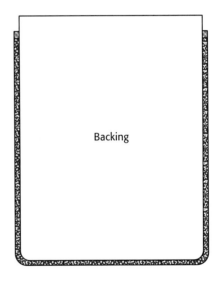

Backing

Ease corners.

43

10. Press under the top and side edges of the backing ½". Fold the excess over itself, wrong sides together, until the top pressed-under edge just meets the plaid strip across the top of the duvet cover; pin the pressed edge in place. The backing should not overlap the top. Topstitch along the pressed-under edges.

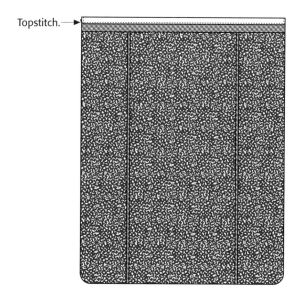

Topstitch. →

11. Fold each toile 3" x 12" strip in half length-wise, right sides together. Stitch along one end and the long edge. Turn the strips to the right side. Position the seam so that it is on the side of the tube; press. Topstitch along the finished end.

12. Lay the raw edge of each step 11 strip ½" above the topstitched edge of the backing, positioning the strip to correspond with the loops on the cover top. Baste the strips in place. Fold the strips over the raw edge and topstitch ¼" from the folded edge.

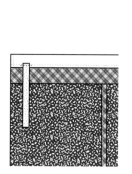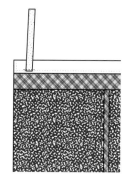

Adding the Pillow Top

1. Refer to steps 2 and 3 of "Making the Duvet Cover" on pages 41 and 42 to sew the remaining covered cording to one long side of each chenille 22½" x 27" rectangle. Stitch the corded rectangles to the sides of the chenille 27" x 45" rectangle.

2. Using the 10" dinner plate, gently round the corners along the top edge of the pillow top. Position the 27" x 88" backing rectangle on the chenille top, right sides together, and round the corners to match.

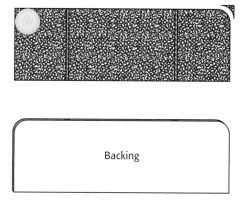

Backing

3. Stitch around the side and top edges, leaving the straight edge open and using a scant ½" seam allowance. Turn the pillow top right side out. Press, gently pulling the chenille slightly to the back. Topstitch 1" from the outside edge of the sides and top to keep the backing from showing on the front.

4. Smooth the bottom edges of the chenille and the backing. Straighten the edge if necessary. Zigzag stitch along the raw edge.

Zigzag along the raw edge.

5. Lay the duvet cover, backing side up, on a large, flat surface. Place the pillow top, chenille side up, over the backing, aligning the pillow-top straight edge with the top folded edge of the backing. Stitch along the top edge with a ⅜" seam allowance.

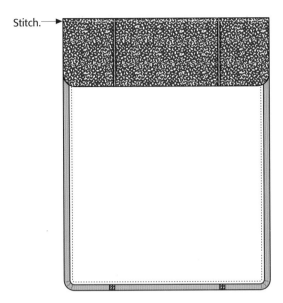

6. Flip the duvet cover over so that the chenille side is up. Press the seam allowance toward the cover. Fold the pillow top over the seam so the backing side is up. Stitch ½" from the seam line, enclosing the seam raw edges.

7. Insert your comforter into the duvet cover. Thread each of the strips at the bottom of the pillow top through both of the rings on the loops of the duvet top and then back through the top ring. Pull up the strip excess to secure the comforter in the cover. Now all you have to do each morning is give the comforter a couple of quick shakes to refluff it, and flip the pillow top over your straightened pillows. Making your bed is a snap!

Reversible Bed Skirt

Finished bed skirt size: Queen

Update your bedroom to fit the season with this reversible bed skirt that goes from dark to light or vice versa with just a flick of the wrist. It's a perfect coordinate for the chenille duvet cover if you use the same plaid and toile fabrics. Note that the bed skirt has an 18" drop, which is a little longer than the standard 14" drop. I made it this size to fit my antique iron bed, but you can adjust the length to meet your own needs.

Materials

- 7⅞ yards of 42"-wide blue plaid for skirt panels
- 5⅞ yards of 108"-wide blue-and-white toile for skirt panels*
- 5 yards of 60"-wide blue ticking for deck (large center piece)

If you use a 42"-wide toile, purchase 7⅞ yards.

Cutting

From the blue ticking, cut on the lengthwise grain:

1 rectangle, 60" x 84"*

From the blue plaid, cut on the lengthwise grain:

2 strips, 19" x 190"

2 strips, 19" x 71"

From the blue-and-white toile, cut on the lengthwise grain:

2 strips, 19" x 190"

2 strips, 19" x 71"

The 60" measurement includes the selvage edges.

**If the toile pattern does not run the length of the fabric, you will need to cut enough strips across the width of the fabric and piece them together to equal the length of the required strips.*

Making the Bed Skirt

1. Turn under one short end of the deck rectangle ½" and zigzag stitch in place. Slightly round the corners of the opposite short end; use a small plate as a guide. Turn under the edges ½" and zigzag stitch them in place.

Turn under edges ½"
and zigzag in place.

2. Pair each plaid 19" x 190" strip with a toile 19" x 190" strip, right sides together. Stitch across the two long edges of each pair; use a ½" seam allowance. Turn the strips right side out; press, keeping the seams along the edges.

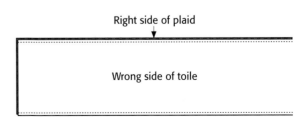

Right side of plaid

Wrong side of toile

3. Turn the short ends of each strip to the inside ½" and topstitch.

4. Join the short ends of the two plaid 19" x 71" strips; use a ½" seam allowance. Repeat for the toile 19" x 71" strips. Refer to steps 2 and 3 to stitch the strips together and finish the ends.

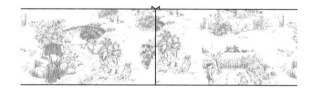

5. Lay one of the 19" x 189" side panels from step 3 on a hard, flat surface, with the plaid side up. Find the center of the upper edge and mark it with a pin. Pin-mark every 5" in each direction. Remove the last three pins on each end of the strip.

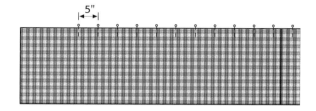

6. Bring the pin on the left of the center pin and the pin on the right of the center pin together behind the center pin to form the first box pleat; pin in place where the two pins meet. Working with the next three pins

on one side of the center pleat, form another pleat in the same manner. Continue in this manner until the entire panel is pleated. There should be an unpleated length at each end, which allows the corners to lie flat. Measure the pleated edge. It should measure 80"; adjust the pleats if necessary.

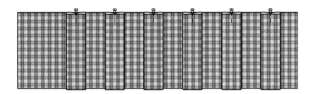

7. Pin the pleats flat at the top and bottom edges, keeping the edges of the strip as straight as possible. Machine baste 1" from the top edge and 2" from the bottom edge.

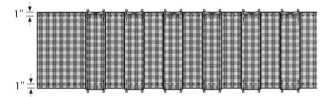

8. Repeat steps 5–7 for the remaining side panel from step 3 and the end panel from step 4, making sure that the plaid side is always facing up before pleating. The end panel should measure 60" after pleating; make any necessary adjustments before basting the pleats in place.

9. On the deck rectangle, mark the center point on each long side and the curved end. Align the center points on the rectangle with the center pleat of each skirt side panel, lapping the upper edge of the panels over the deck rectangle 1½"; topstitch. Repeat with the end panel, overlapping the ends with the ends of the side panels. Remove the basting.

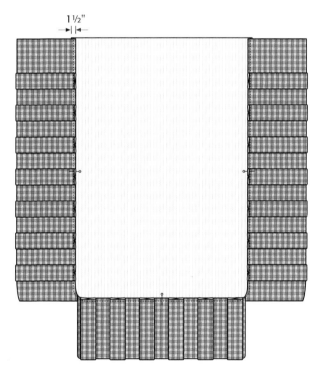

Floral Bouquet Quilt

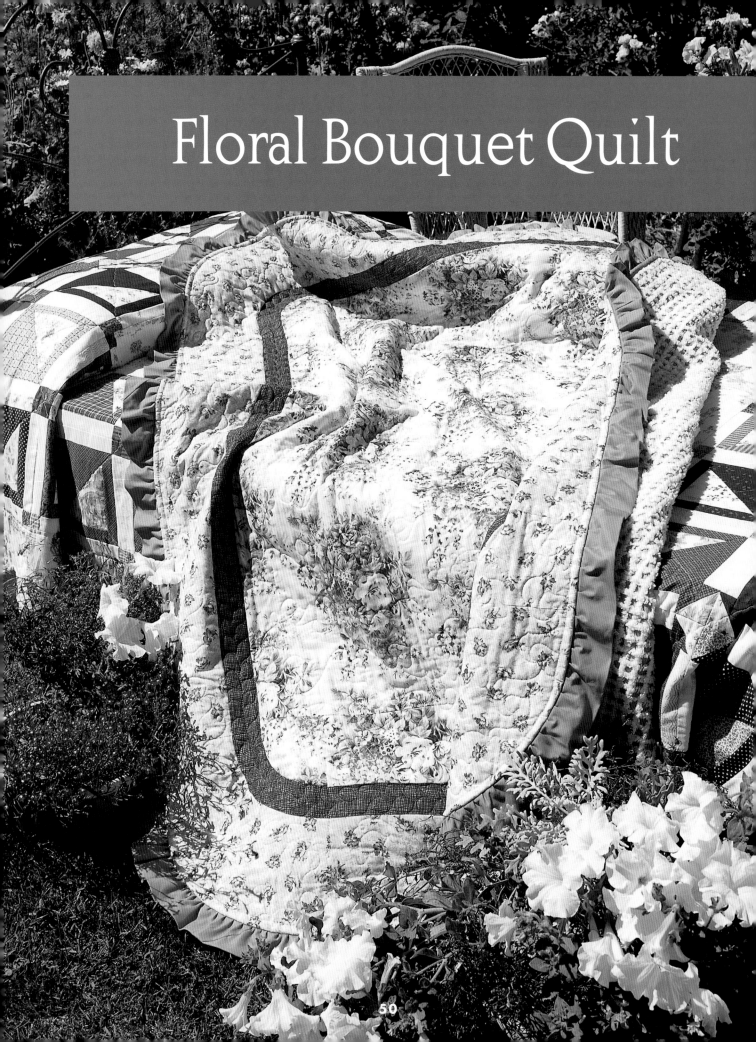

There isn't anything better than picking a bouquet of roses from my garden,

but if I had to choose an alternative, selecting one of the many beautiful floral fabrics available

at my quilt shop would be my choice. This is the perfect throw for showing off a favorite large-scale floral.

Backed with chenille, you'll find it just too cozy to share.

Materials

Yardages are based on 42"-wide fabrics unless otherwise noted.

- 2⅛ yards of large-scale blue floral for quilt-top center
- 1⅞ yards of coordinating small-scale blue floral for outer border
- ⅞ yard of dark blue print for inner border
- 4 yards of 45"-wide blue-and-white cotton chenille for backing
- 2⅜ yards of medium blue solid for ruffle and binding
- 64" x 82" piece of batting
- 13½ yards of thin, strong cord or crochet thread

Cutting

All measurements include ¼"-wide seam allowances.

From the dark blue print, cut:

5 strips, 2½" x 42"; trim 2 strips to 2½" x 30½"

4 of template B (page 56)

From the large-scale blue floral, cut:

1 rectangle, 40" x 48"

2 strips, 5½" x 30½"

4 of template A (page 55)

From the small-scale blue floral, cut:

2 strips, 7½" x 48", from the *lengthwise* grain

2 strips, 7½" x 30½", from the *lengthwise* grain

4 of template C (page 57)

Making the Quilt Top

1. Join the three dark blue 2½" x 42" strips end to end; use a diagonal seam (refer to joining binding strips in "Binding" on page 91). From the pieced strip, cut two strips, 2½" x 48". Sew the strips to the sides of the large-scale floral 40" x 48" rectangle. Sew a small-scale floral 7½" x 48" strip to the dark blue strips.

2. Fold each template A, B, and C piece in half, right sides together, to mark the center points of the edges to be sewn together; crease along the fold.

3. Make the corner units. With right sides together and centers aligned, pin each template A piece to a template B piece at the center points. Beginning on one end, stitch along the curved edge, easing the fabric as necessary. Press the seams toward the B

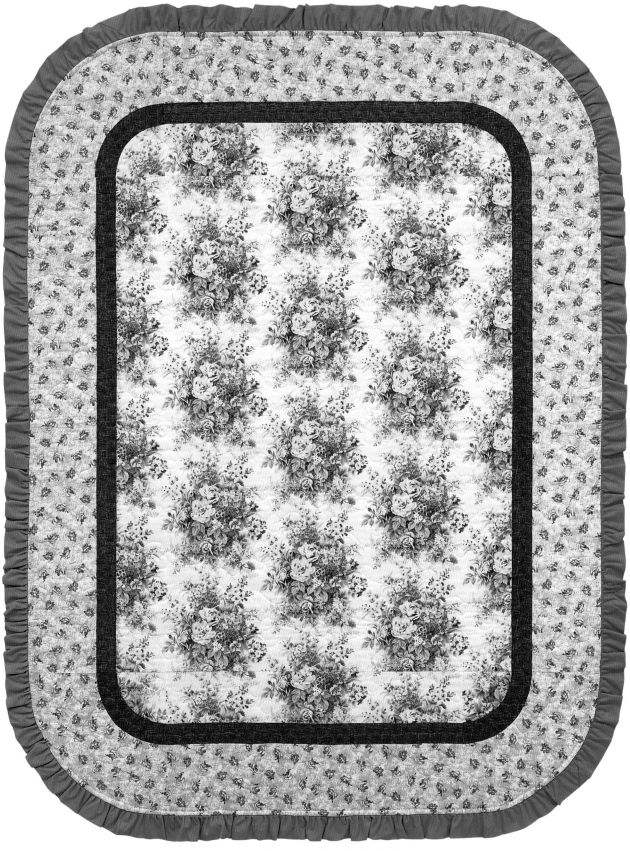

Finished quilt size: 62" x 80"

pieces. Repeat to stitch each template C piece to a template B piece. Press the seams toward the C pieces.

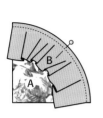

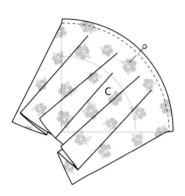

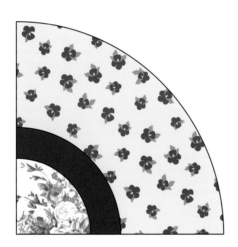

4. Sew a large-scale floral 5½" x 30½" strip to each dark blue 2½" x 30½" strip. Sew a small-scale floral 7½" x 30½" strip to the other edge of the dark blue strips. Stitch a corner unit to each side of these units as shown, aligning the colors. Make two.

Make 2.

5. Sew a unit from step 4 to the top and bottom edges of the unit from step 1 as shown.

Finishing the Quilt

1. Layer the quilt top with batting and backing; baste (refer to "Layering the Quilt" on page 90).

2. Machine quilt as desired (refer to "Quilting" on page 91).

3. Refer to "Bias Binding" on page 92 to cut and join enough 5½"-wide bias strips from the medium blue solid to measure approximately 468" for the ruffle. Also from the medium blue solid, cut and join enough 2"-wide bias strips to measure approximately 306" for the binding.

4. With right sides together, stitch the ends of the ruffle strip together to form a circle. Press the ruffle strip in half lengthwise, wrong sides together. Set your machine for a wide zigzag stitch. Place the cord or crochet thread ⅜" from the raw edges of the strip. You will need some excess cord at the beginning and end of where you start and stop stitching. Zigzag over the cord, leaving the excess cord unstitched. Be careful not to catch the cord in the stitching.

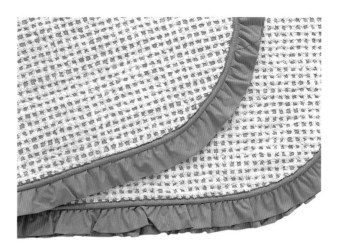

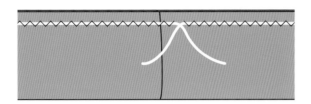

5. Pin-mark the center of each side, top, and bottom edge of the quilt top. Fold the ruffle strip in half and then in half again; pin-mark the folds. With the quilt top right side up and raw edges aligned, pin the ruffle strip to the quilt at the center points, matching the pin marks. Pull on the cord ends to adjust the gathers to fit between the pin marks. Evenly distribute the gathers; pin the gathered strip to the edges of the quilt top. Baste ¼" from the raw edges. Remove the cord.

6. Press the binding strip in half, wrong sides together. With the raw edges aligned, place the binding strip over the ruffle and stitch it in place. Turn the binding to the back of the quilt and topstitch it in place. Remove any visible basting stitches.

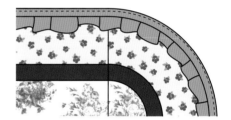

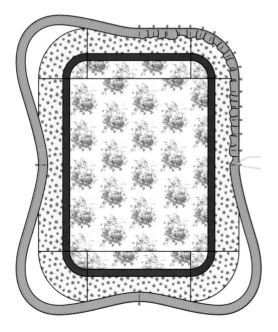

Corner Unit Pattern

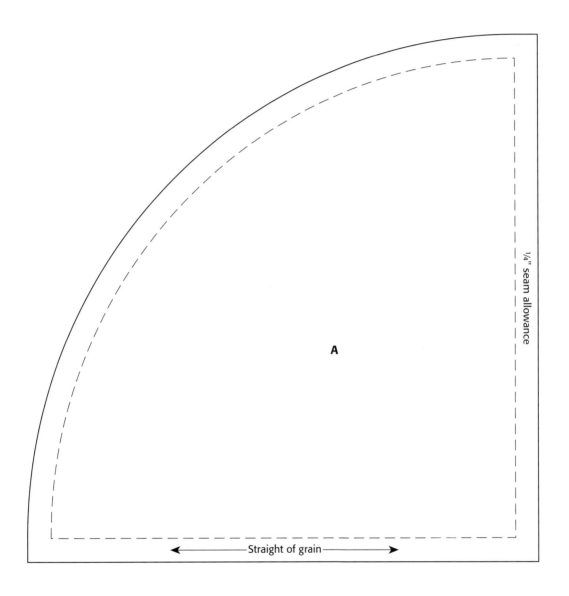

A

¼" seam allowance

Straight of grain

Corner Unit Pattern

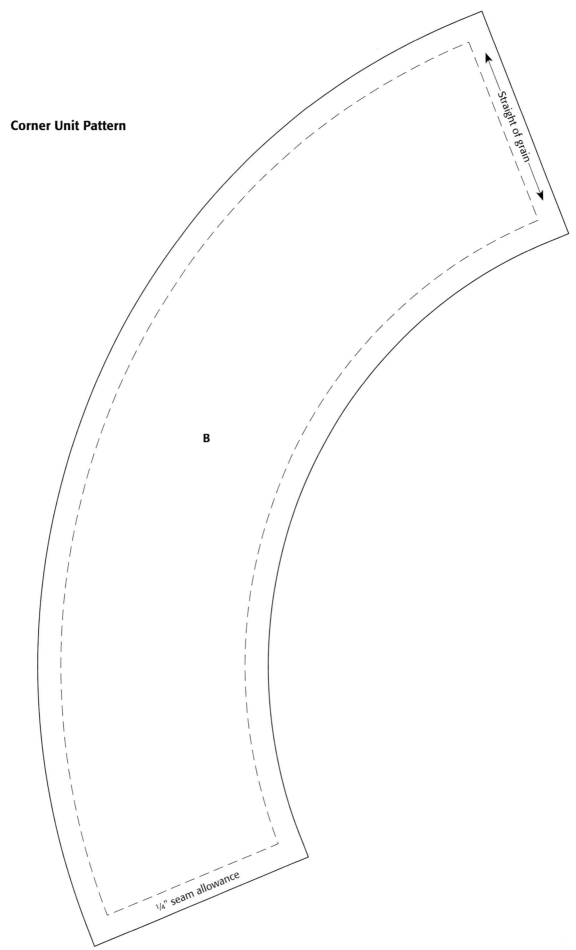

Straight of grain

B

¼" seam allowance

Corner Unit Pattern

Enlarge pattern 200%.

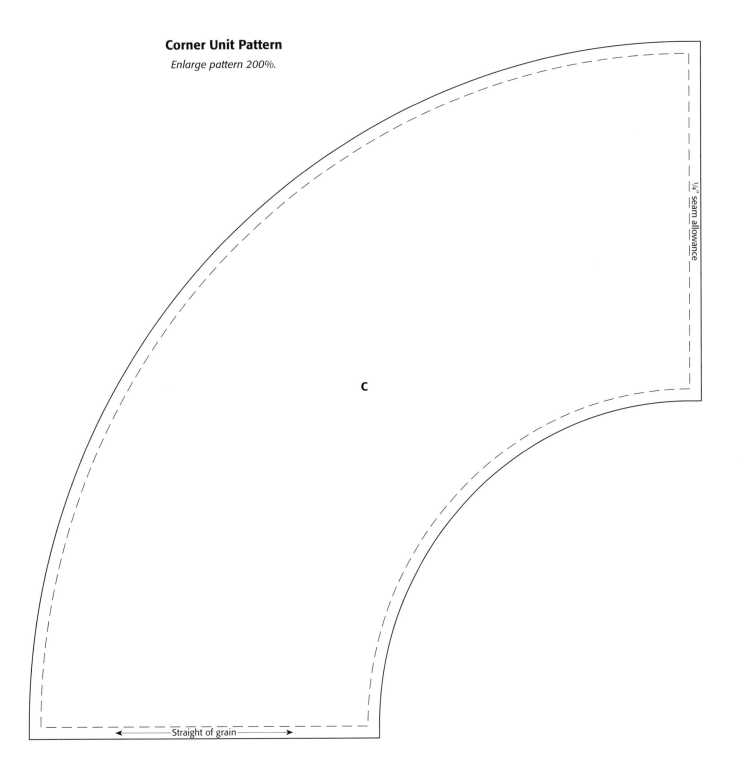

C

¼" seam allowance

Straight of grain

Maggie's "Headboard"

This project is for my sister who lives in earthquake country. For years she has had a blank wall at the head of her bed. I have repeatedly made tactful suggestions as to what would look good in that spot, but I'm always reminded that if you live in earthquake country, you should not put anything on the wall that could fall and hurt you. She can't object to this soft, quilted headboard.

Materials

Yardages are based on 42"-wide fabrics.

- ¾ yard of large-scale white-with-red print for outer border
- ⅝ yard *total* of assorted reds for blocks and inner pieced border
- ½ yard of small-scale white-with-red print for block background
- ¼ yard *total* of assorted white-with-red prints for blocks and inner border
- ¼ yard of deep red for blocks
- 1½ yards of muslin for headboard-top backing
- 1½ yards of red check for ruffle
- 1½ yards of fabric for backing
- 1 yard of fabric for binding
- 52" x 52" square of batting
- 8½ yards of thin, strong cord or crochet thread

Cutting

From the deep red, cut:

3 strips, 1½" x 42", crosscut the strips into:

8 rectangles, 1½" x 5½"

8 rectangles, 1½" x 4½"

8 squares, 1½" x 1½"

From the small-scale white-with-red print, cut:

4 strips, 1½" x 42"; crosscut the strips into:

8 rectangles, 1½" x 5½"

8 rectangles, 1½" x 4½"

24 rectangles, 1½" x 2½"

8 squares, 1½" x 1½"

1 strip, 2⅞" x 42"; crosscut the strip into 8 squares, 2⅞" x 2⅞"

From the assorted reds, cut a *total* of:

8 squares, 2⅞" x 2⅞"

8 squares, 2½" x 2½"

44 rectangles, 1½" x 6½"

From the assorted white-with-red prints, cut a *total* of:

60 squares, 1½" x 1½"

From the large-scale white-with-red print, cut:

3 strips, 6½" x 42"

From the muslin, cut:

2 rectangles, 36" x 52"

From the backing fabric, cut:

1 rectangle, 36" x 52"

From the batting, cut:

2 rectangles, 36" x 52"

2 strips, 8" x 18"

2 strips, 8" x 34"

Making the Tulip Blocks

1. Sew a deep red 1½" square to one side of each background 1½" square. Stitch a background 1½" x 2½" rectangle to one long side of each pair as shown. Make eight units. Each unit should measure 2½" square.

Make 8.

2. Pair each assorted red 2⅞" square with a background 2⅞" square, right sides together, with the background squares on top. Draw a diagonal line from corner to corner on the

59

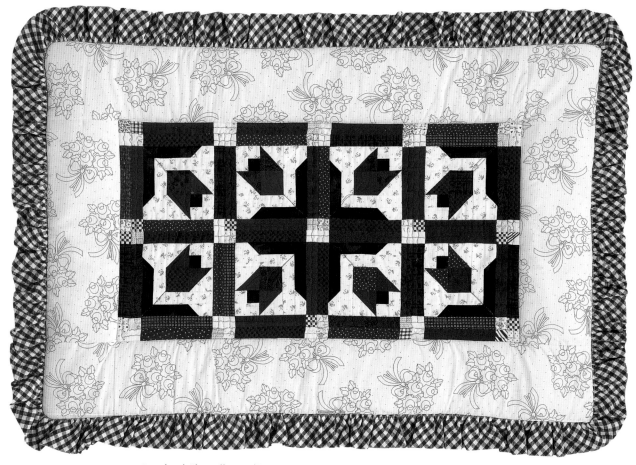

Finished "headboard" size: 51" x 35" ◆ Finished block size: 8"

wrong side of each background square. Stitch ¼" from each side of the drawn lines. Cut the squares apart on the drawn lines and press open the 16 resulting triangle squares.

Make 16.

3. Join one assorted red 2½" square, two matching triangle squares from step 2, and one unit from step 1 into two rows as shown. Stitch the units in each row together, and then stitch the rows together. Make eight units.

Make 8.

4. Sew a background 1½" x 4½" rectangle to the bottom of each unit from step 3, and then sew a background 1½" x 5½" rectangle to the left side of each unit as shown.

5. Place a background 1½" x 2½" rectangle at one end of each deep red 1½" x 4½" rectangle as shown, right sides together. Draw a diagonal line on each background rectangle that goes from the lower left corner to the upper edge where the two rectangles intersect. Sew on the drawn line, and then trim

¼" from the stitching line. Press the background rectangle up. The pieced rectangles should measure 1½" x 5½".

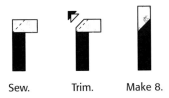

Sew.   Trim.   Make 8.

6. Place a background 1½" x 2½" rectangle at one end of each deep red 1½" x 5½" rectangle as shown, right sides together. Draw a diagonal line on each background rectangle that goes from the lower right corner to the upper edge where the two rectangles intersect. Sew on the drawn line, and then trim ¼" from the stitching line. Press the background rectangle up. The pieced rectangles should measure 1½" x 6½".

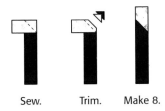

Sew.   Trim.   Make 8.

7. Stitch the pieced rectangles from step 5 to the bottom of each unit from step 4 as shown. Stitch the pieced rectangles from step 6 to the left side of each unit as shown.

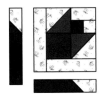

8. Sew an assorted red 1½" x 6½" rectangle to the right and left sides of each unit from step 7 as shown. Sew an assorted white-with-red print 1½" square to each end of the remaining assorted red 1½" x 6½" rectangles. Stitch one of these pieced rectangles to the top and bottom of each unit as shown. Set the remaining pieced rectangles aside for the inner border. Square up each block, if necessary, so that it measures 8½" x 8½".

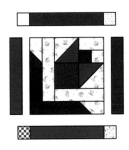

Make 8.

Assembling the Headboard Top

1. Arrange the Tulip blocks into two horizontal rows as shown. Sew the blocks in each row together. Press the seams of each row in opposite directions. Stitch the rows together. Press the seam in one direction.

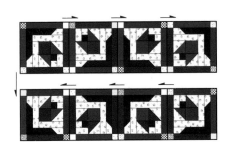

2. To make the inner side border strips, join two of the pieced rectangles you set aside in step 8 of "Making the Tulip Blocks" end to end to make one long strip. Make two. To make the inner top and bottom border strips, join four of the remaining pieced rectangles end to end to make one long strip. Stitch an assorted white-with-red print 1½" square to each end of the strip. Make two.

Side Border
Make 2.

Top/Bottom Border
Make 2.

3. Refer to the headboard assembly diagram to stitch the inner side borders to the headboard top. Stitch the inner top and bottom borders to the top and bottom edges of the headboard top.

4. Refer to "Adding Borders" on page 87 to measure the headboard top for straight-cut outer borders. From the large-scale white-with-red print 6½" x 42" strips, cut two strips the length needed for the side borders. Stitch the borders to the sides of the headboard top. Measure the headboard top for the top and bottom borders. Cut two strips the length needed from the remaining outer-border strips and stitch the strips to the top and bottom edges of the headboard top.

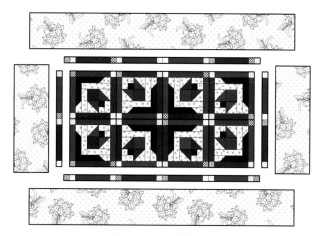

Headboard Assembly Diagram

Finishing the Headboard

1. Lay one muslin rectangle on a flat surface. Center a batting rectangle over the muslin rectangle. Center the headboard top over the batting rectangle, right side up. Refer to "Layering the Quilt" on page 90 to baste the layers together through the Tulip blocks only. Machine quilt the Tulip blocks as desired, leaving the inner and outer borders unquilted. Stitch in the ditch between the blocks and inner border.

2. Fold back the unquilted top and bottom borders on the headboard top and lay an 8" x 34" batting strip over the previous batting. Fold back the unquilted side borders and fill in the space between the top and bottom batting strips with the 8" x 18" batting strips. Fold the top back over the batting strips and smooth it in place; baste the border layers together. Stitch in the ditch between the inner and outer borders, catching the second layer of batting. Machine baste along the outside edge of the headboard top to hold all of the layers together.

3. Using a water-soluble fabric marker, mark a 2"-wide crosshatch grid on the remaining muslin rectangle. Lay the 36" x 52" backing piece wrong side up on a flat surface. Center the remaining batting rectangle and then the

marked muslin rectangle over the backing. Baste the layers together. With the muslin side up, machine quilt on the marked lines.

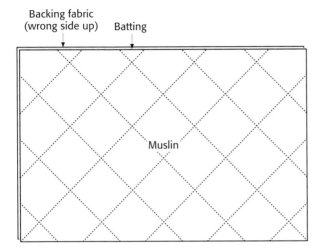

Backing fabric (wrong side up) Batting

Muslin

4. Refer to "Adding a Hanging Sleeve" on page 91 to make a hanging sleeve and pin it to the upper edge of the back of the headboard.

5. Lay the quilted backing, wrong side up, on a flat surface. Center the quilted top over the backing, right side up. Machine baste along the outer edges.

6. Refer to "Bias Binding" on page 92 to cut and join enough 6"-wide bias strips from the red check to measure approximately 300" for the ruffle. From the binding fabric, cut and join enough 3½"-wide bias strips to measure approximately 180".

7. With right sides together, stitch the ends of the ruffle strip together to form a circle. Press the ruffle strip in half lengthwise, wrong sides together. Set your machine for a wide zigzag stitch. Place the cord or crochet thread ⅜" from the raw edges of the strip. You will need some excess cord at the beginning and end of where you start and stop stitching. Zigzag over the cord, leaving the excess cord unstitched. Be careful not to catch the cord in the stitching.

8. Pin-mark the center of each side, top, and bottom edge of the headboard top. Fold the ruffle strip in half and then in half again;

pin-mark the folds. With the headboard top right side up and the raw edges aligned, pin the ruffle strip to the headboard at the center points, matching the pin marks. Pull on the cord ends to adjust the gathers to fit between the pin marks. Evenly distribute the gathers; pin the gathered strip to the edges of the headboard, rounding the corners with the ruffle strip. Baste ¼" from the raw edges. Remove the cord.

9. Press the binding strip in half, wrong sides together. With the raw edges aligned, lay the binding over the ruffle and stitch it in place with a ½"-wide seam allowance and a slightly longer than normal stitch length.

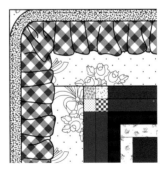

10. Smooth out the ruffle folded edge so that it is facing away from the headboard center; stitch close to the seam line, being careful not to catch the binding folded edge in the stitching.

11. Turn the binding to the back of the headboard and hand or machine stitch it in place. Remove any visible basting stitches.

Red Tulips Quilt

Every day feels like summer vacation when you awake from a nap under this cheerful throw. Shades of red and white, another winning color combination that has been a quilter's classic since the 1800s, are just as smart today as they were when they were first achieved with muslin and Turkey red thread.

Materials

Yardages are based on 42"-wide fabrics.

- 2 yards of red check for ruffle and binding
- 1⅝ yards of large-scale white-with-red print for outer border
- 1½ yards *total* of assorted reds for blocks and inner pieced border
- ⅞ yard of small-scale white-with-red print for block background
- ½ yard of deep red for blocks
- ½ yard *total* of assorted white-with-red prints for inner pieced border
- 3½ yards of fabric for backing
- 54" x 70" piece of batting
- 12 yards of thin, strong cord or crochet thread

Cutting

All measurements include ¼"-wide seam allowances.

From the deep red, cut:

7 strips, 1½" x 42"; crosscut the strips into:
24 rectangles, 1½" x 5½"
24 rectangles, 1½" x 4½"
24 squares, 1½" x 1½"

From the small-scale white-with-red print, cut:

2 strips, 2⅞" x 42"; crosscut the strips into 24 squares, 2⅞" x 2⅞"
12 strips, 1½" x 42", crosscut the strips into:
24 rectangles, 1½" x 5½"
24 rectangles, 1½" x 4½"
72 rectangles, 1½" x 2½"
24 squares, 1½" x 1½"

From the assorted reds, cut:

24 squares, 2⅞" x 2⅞"
24 squares, 2½" x 2½"
116 rectangles, 1½" x 6½"

From the assorted white-with-red prints, cut:

140 squares, 1½" x 1½"

From the large-scale white-with-red print, cut:

6 strips, 8½" x 42"

Making the Tulip Blocks

Refer to "Making the Tulip Blocks" on page 59 and the illustration below to make 24 Tulip blocks.

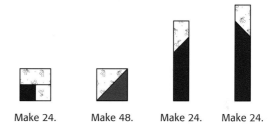

Make 24.   Make 48.   Make 24.   Make 24.

Make 68.

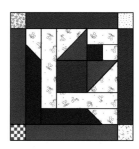

Make 24.

Finished quilt size: 53" x 69" ◆ Finished block size: 8"

Assembling the Quilt Top

1. Refer to the quilt assembly diagram to arrange the Tulip blocks into six horizontal rows of four blocks each as shown. Sew the blocks in each row together. Press the seams in opposite directions from row to row. Stitch the rows together. Press the seams in one direction.

2. To make the inner side border strips, join six of the units you set aside in step 8 of "Making the Tulip Blocks" end to end to make one long strip. Make two. To make the inner top and bottom border strips, join four of the remaining units end to end to make one long strip. Stitch an assorted white-with-red print 1½" square to each end of the strip. Make two.

3. Refer to the quilt assembly diagram to stitch the side borders to the quilt top. Stitch the top and bottom borders to the top and bottom edges of the quilt top.

4. Refer to "Adding Borders" on page 87 to measure the quilt top for straight-cut outer borders. Sew the large-scale white-with-red print 8½" x 42" strips together, end to end. From the long strip, cut two strips the length needed for the side borders. Stitch the borders to the sides of the quilt top. Measure the quilt top for the top and bottom borders. From the remaining white-with-red print pieced strip, cut two strips the length needed for the top and bottom borders. Stitch the strips to the top and bottom edges of the quilt top.

Quilt Assembly Diagram

Finishing the Quilt

1. Layer the quilt top with batting and backing; baste (refer to "Layering the Quilt" on page 90).

2. Hand or machine quilt as desired (refer to "Quilting" on page 91).

3. Refer to "Bias Binding" on page 92 to cut and join enough 6"-wide bias strips from the red check to measure approximately 420" for the ruffle. Also from the red check, cut and join enough 2"-wide bias strips to measure approximately 234" for the binding.

4. With right sides together, stitch the ends of the ruffle strip together to form a circle. Press the ruffle strip in half lengthwise, wrong sides together.

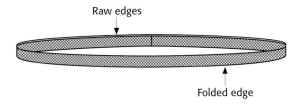

Raw edges

Folded edge

5. Set your machine for a wide zigzag stitch. Place the cord or crochet thread ⅜" from the raw edges of the strip. You will need some excess cord at the beginning and end of where you start and stop stitching. Zigzag over the cord, leaving the excess cord unstitched. Be careful not to catch the cord in the stitching.

6. Pin-mark the center of each side, top, and bottom edge of the quilt top. Fold the ruffle strip in half and then in half again; pin-mark the folds. With the quilt top right side up and raw edges aligned, pin the ruffle strip to the quilt at the center points, matching the pin marks. Pull on the cord ends to adjust the gathers to fit between the pin marks. Evenly distribute the gathers; pin the gathered strip to the edges of the quilt top, slightly rounding the corners. Baste ¼" from the raw edges. Remove the cord.

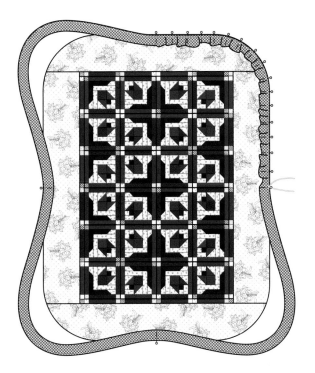

68

7. Press the binding strip in half, wrong sides together. With the raw edges even, lay the binding over the ruffle and stitch it in place.

8. Turn the binding to the back of the quilt and topstitch it in place. Remove any visible basting stitches.

Star Pillow

Finished pillow size: 14" x 14"

Plan to make a whole galaxy of these pillows. It's fun to vary the sizes, fabrics, and trims to make each one different, just like the stars in the sky.

Materials

◆ ½ yard of 45"-wide chenille

◆ 2 yards of decorator trim

◆ 1 bag of polyester fiberfill

Making the Pillow

1. Enlarge the star pattern below to the percentage indicated.

2. Using the enlarged pattern, cut two star shapes from the chenille for the pillow front and back.

3. With the lip of the trim aligned with the fabric raw edge, machine baste the trim to the right side of one of the star pieces. Use a *scant* ¼" seam allowance.

4. With right sides together, stitch the front to the back, stitching just inside the row of basting stitches. Leave a 3" opening on one straight side of a star point.

5. Turn the pillow to the right side and smooth out the edges. Fill the pillow with fiberfill until it is the desired firmness.

6. Slipstitch the opening closed.

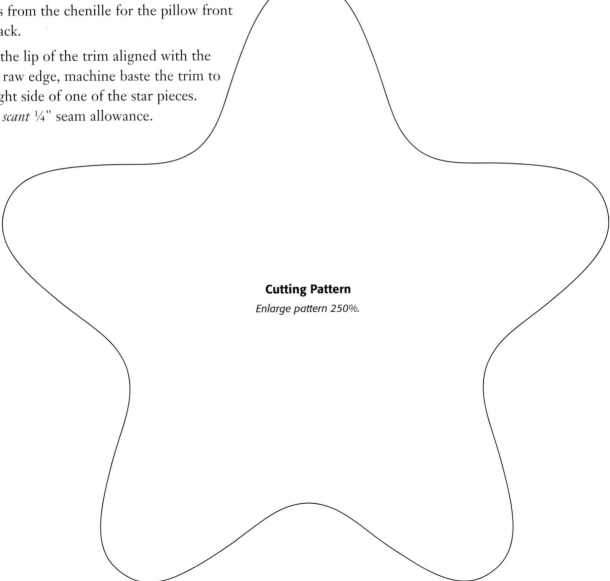

Cutting Pattern
Enlarge pattern 250%.

Once in a Blue Moon Pillow

Finished pillow size: 14" round

This pillow is quick and easy and works well with its partner, "Star Pillow" (page 70). Together they add lots of decorator punch to any spot in your home. Envision looking at the moon and stars on a warm summer evening, comforted by several of these pillows and a light throw.

Materials

Yardages are based on 42"-wide fabrics.

- ¾ yard of light blue plaid for front and back
- ½ yard of dark blue print for appliqué
- 8½" x 11" rectangle of lightweight paper-backed fusible web
- Pencil or fabric marker
- 1 package of white Chenille by the Inch (see "Embellishing with Faux Chenille" on page 86)
- Chenille brush
- 14"-diameter pillow form

Cutting

Measurement includes ¼"-wide seam allowance.

From the blue plaid, cut:

2 squares, 20" x 20"

Making the Pillow

1. Enlarge the moon pattern on page 74 to the percentage indicated.

2. Using the enlarged pattern, trace the moon onto the paper side of the fusible web rectangle. Follow the manufacturer's instructions to fuse the rectangle to the wrong side of the dark blue print. Cut out the shape. Transfer the eye marking to the right side of the shape with a pencil or fabric marker.

3. Press one of the blue plaid squares in half lengthwise and crosswise. The point where the lines cross is the pillow center. Remove the paper backing from the appliqué and center it on the square. Fuse the appliqué in place. Transfer the eye marking to the appliqué with a pencil or fabric marker.

4. Follow the manufacturer's instructions and "Embellishing with Faux Chenille" on page 86 to prepare and apply the Chenille by the Inch to the appliqué outer edges and the eye marking. Brush the chenille with the chenille brush to fluff it.

5. With right sides together, stitch the appliquéd square to the remaining plaid square around the outer edges, leaving a 7" opening on one side. Trim the corners and turn the pillow covering to the right side. Insert the pillow form into the opening, and then slipstitch the opening closed.

6. Tie each corner in a knot.

Appliqué Pattern
Enlarge pattern 125%.

White Carnations
for a Blue Lady Pillow

Finished pillow size: 16" x 16"

*Now tell me, who could resist the charm of this pillow? It's one of my favorite looks—
a blue-and-white Basket block filled with chenille carnations.*

Materials

Yardages are based on 42"-wide fabrics.

◆ ¼ yard *total* of assorted creams for basket background

◆ ⅝ yard of muslin for pillow-top backing

◆ 1 fat quarter of blue fabric for basket

◆ 1 fat quarter of floral print for basket flowers

◆ ⅞ yard of fabric for backing

◆ 16" x 16" square of batting

◆ 1 package *each* of blue and white Chenille by the Inch (see "Embellishing with Faux Chenille" on page 86)

◆ Chenille brush

◆ 16" x 16" pillow form

Cutting

All measurements include ¼"-wide seam allowances.

From the blue, cut:

1 square, 12⅞" x 12⅞"; cut the square in half once diagonally to yield 2 triangles. You will use 1 triangle and have 1 left over.

1 rectangle, 2½" x 13"

1 rectangle, 2½" x 11"

1 rectangle, 2½" x 4½"

1 square, 2½" x 2½"

From the floral print, cut:

1 square, 8⅞" x 8⅞"; cut the square in half once diagonally to yield 2 triangles. You will use 1 triangle and have 1 left over.

From the assorted creams, cut a *total* of:

2 strips, 2½" x 42"; crosscut the strips into:

1 rectangle, 2½" x 16½"

1 rectangle, 2½" x 14½"

2 rectangles, 2½" x 10½"

1 square, 4½" x 4½"

From the muslin, cut:

1 square, 17" x 17"

From the backing fabric, cut:

1 rectangle, 16½" x 25"

1 rectangle, 16½" x 15"

Making the Pillow

1. Follow steps 1–5 of "Making the Basket Blocks" on page 21 to make a 16½" square Basket block for the pillow top.

2. Transfer the design on page 27 to the block. Follow the manufacturer's instructions and "Embellishing with Faux Chenille" on page 86 to prepare and apply the chenille strips to the design. Fluff the chenille with the chenille brush.

3. Lay the muslin square on a flat surface. Place the batting square over the muslin square. Center the pillow top over the batting square, right side up. Refer to "Layering the Quilt" on page 90 to baste the layers together. Hand or machine quilt as desired.

4. Fold the backing 16½" x 25" rectangle in half, wrong sides together, to form a 16½" x 12½" rectangle. Fold the backing 16½" x 15" rectangle in half, wrong sides together, to form a 16½" x 7½" rectangle. Press the folded edge of each backing piece.

5. Lap the folded edge of the 16½" x 12½" backing piece over the 16½" x 7½" backing piece by 3½" to create a 16½" x 16½" backing piece. Pin the pieces together along the folded edges.

6. Center the pillow top, wrong side up, over the backing piece. Stitch completely around the outer edges. Trim the corners and turn the pillow cover to the right side through the backing opening. Insert the pillow form through the backing opening.

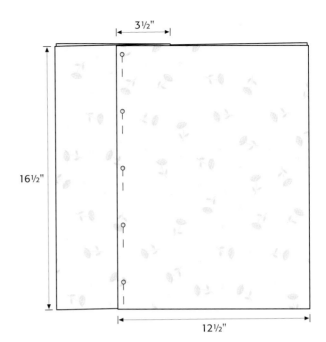

Summers on the Farm Quilt

I remember my childhood summers on the farm when our hot, busy days were interrupted by a cool dip in the fishing hole, followed by sunning ourselves on a favorite quilt—kind of like this one. Make it from red and blue country homespun plaids and it will always be ready for impromptu picnics at the beach or relaxing under a cool shade tree.

Materials

Yardages are based on 42"-wide fabrics.

- 3¾ yards of dark blue plaid for blocks, outer border, and binding
- 1½ yards of red plaid for blocks and inner border
- 1½ yards of light blue plaid for blocks
- ⅞ yard of yellow plaid for blocks
- ¼ yard of dark red fabric for blocks
- 4¾ yards of fabric for backing
- 80" x 80" square of batting
- 5½" x 5½" square of template plastic

Cutting

All measurements include ¼"-wide seam allowances.

From the dark blue plaid, cut:

8 strips, 6½" x 42"

4 strips, 5½" x 42"; crosscut the strips into 24 rectangles, 5½" x 6½"

5 strips, 3⅜" x 42"; crosscut the strips into 52 squares, 3⅜" x 3⅜"

4 strips, 3" x 42"; crosscut the strips into 52 squares, 3" x 3"

8 strips, 2½" x 42"

From the red plaid, cut:

7 strips, 3⅜" x 42"; crosscut the strips into 76 squares, 3⅜" x 3⅜"

4 strips, 3" x 42"; crosscut the strips into 52 squares, 3" x 3"

8 strips, 1½" x 42"

From the light blue plaid, cut:

15 strips, 3" x 42"; crosscut the strips into 100 rectangles, 3" x 5½"

From the dark red, cut:

2 strips, 3" x 42"; crosscut the strips into 25 squares, 3" x 3"

From the yellow plaid, cut:

3 strips, 3⅜" x 42"; crosscut the strips into 24 squares, 3⅜" x 3⅜"

5 strips, 3" x 42"; crosscut the strips into 48 rectangles, 3" x 4"

Making the Farmer's Daughter Blocks

1. Pair each of the 52 dark blue plaid 3⅜" squares with a red plaid 3⅜" square, right sides together, with the red squares on top. Lightly draw a diagonal line from corner to corner on the wrong side of each red square. Stitch ¼" from each side of the drawn lines. Cut the squares apart on the drawn lines and press open the 104 resulting triangle squares.

Make 104.

2. Sew a dark blue plaid 3" square to 52 triangle squares from step 1 as shown.

Make 52.

Finished quilt size: 74" x 74" ◆ Finished block size: 12½"

3. Sew a red plaid 3" square to the remaining triangle squares from step 1.

Make 52.

4. Sew the units from steps 2 and 3 together as shown.

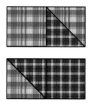

Make 52.

5. Arrange four units from step 4, four light blue plaid 3" x 5½" rectangles, and one dark red 3" square into three horizontal rows as shown. Be careful to orient the step 4 units correctly. Stitch the pieces in each row together, and then stitch the rows together to complete the block. Make 13.

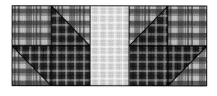

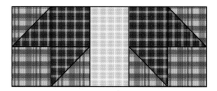

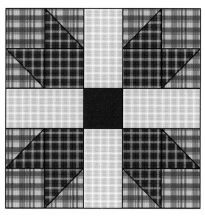

Make 13.

Making the Duck and Duckling Blocks

1. Pair each yellow 3⅜" square with a red plaid 3⅜" square, right sides together, with the yellow squares on top. Draw a diagonal line from corner to corner on the wrong side of each yellow square. Stitch ¼" from each side of the drawn lines. Cut the squares apart on the drawn lines and press open the resulting 48 triangle squares.

Make 48.

2. With right sides together, sew a triangle square from step 1 to each yellow plaid 3" x 4" rectangle as shown.

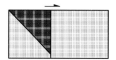

3. Sew the units from step 2 together in pairs as shown, carefully matching the outside edges.

 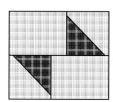

4. Clip the seam allowance just through the seam line between the two triangle squares of each unit. Press the seams away from the triangle squares.

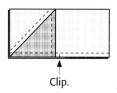 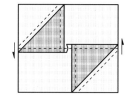

Clip.

5. Cut the 5½" square of template plastic in half diagonally to make a triangle template.

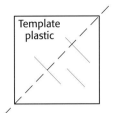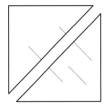

6. Place the template on the wrong side of each pieced rectangle, with the corner of the template over one of the triangle squares as shown. Draw the diagonal line as shown. Repeat in the opposite corner of each unit, again placing the corner of the template over the triangle square.

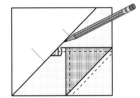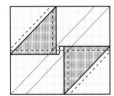

Mark stitching lines.

7. With right sides together, place each of the marked units on a dark blue plaid 5½" x 6½" rectangle. Sew on each of the drawn lines, and then cut between them. Press the seams toward the large blue triangles. Make 48.

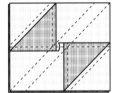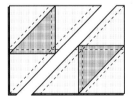

Make 48.

8. Arrange four units from step 7, four light blue plaid 3" x 5½" rectangles, and one dark red 3" square into three horizontal rows as shown. Be careful to orient the step 7 units correctly. Stitch the pieces in each row together, and then stitch the rows together to complete the block. Make 12.

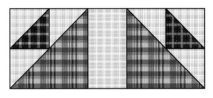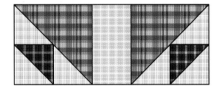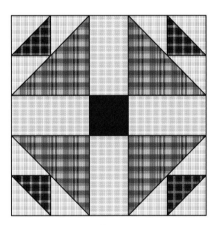

Make 12.

Assembling the Quilt Top

1. Refer to the quilt assembly diagram to arrange the Farmer's Daughter blocks and Duck and Ducklings blocks into five horizontal rows as shown. Sew the blocks in each row together. Press the seams in opposite directions from row to row. Stitch the rows together. Press the seams in one direction.

2. Refer to "Adding Borders" on page 87 to measure the quilt top for straight-cut borders. Piece the red plaid 1½" x 42" strips together. From this long strip, cut two strips the length needed for the quilt sides. Stitch the borders to the sides of the quilt top. Measure the quilt top for the top and bottom borders. From the remaining red plaid pieced strip, cut two strips the length needed and stitch the strips to the top and bottom edges of the quilt top. Repeat with the dark blue plaid 6½" x 42" strips for the outer border.

Finishing the Quilt

1. Layer the quilt top with batting and backing; baste (refer to "Layering the Quilt" on page 90).

2. Hand or machine quilt as desired (refer to "Quilting" on page 91).

3. Add a hanging sleeve, if desired (refer to "Adding a Hanging Sleeve" on page 91).

4. Bind the quilt edges (refer to "Binding" on page 91).

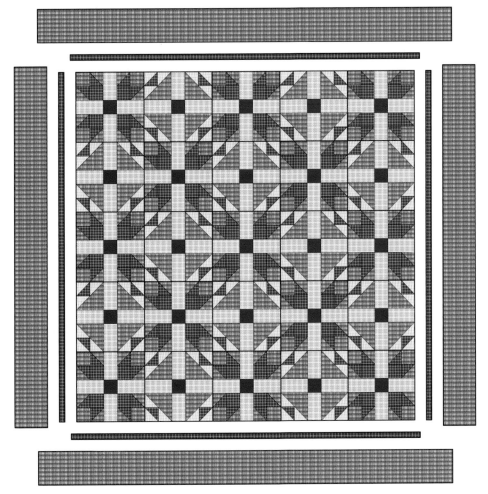

Quilt Assembly Diagram

Quilt Storage Bag

When the frost appears on the pumpkins, it's time to put your summertime quilts away. Cotton storage bags that coordinate with your quilts are just the place to keep quilts clean and safe until next year, and they're a great way to use up your leftover scraps. The bag shown here is for "Summers on the Farm Quilt." I used left-over backing fabric for the bag and made an extra block that I stitched to the outside for a pocket that holds a small pillow. If you don't have large pieces of leftover fabric, just piece scraps together until the piece is large enough to cut the rectangles. The instructions here will make a plain bag that fits up to a queen-size quilt.

Materials

- 2 rectangles, 24" x 36", for bag
- 3 yards of cotton cord for drawstring
- 2 large wood beads (optional)

If you want to add a block pocket like the one shown in the photo, make an extra block and sew it to the bag front before you stitch the front and back rectangles together.

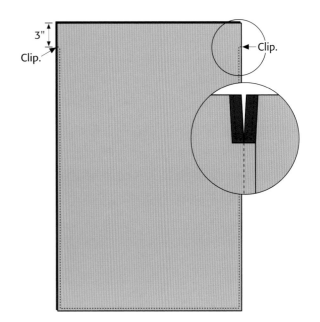

Making the Bag

1. Pin the rectangles right sides together. Begin stitching 3" from the upper edge; backstitch. Stitch down the side, across the bottom, and up the other side, ending 3" from the upper edge; backstitch. Set your machine for a zigzag stitch and stitch the seam allowance edges together to finish them.

2. Clip into the seam allowance directly above where you began and ended stitching. Press under the seam allowance on each side above the stitching line ¼". Stitch the seam allowance in place as shown, beginning on one side and continuing up the other side.

3. Press under the top edges ¼", and then 1½" to form a casing for the cord. Stitch along the pressed-under edge. Turn the bag right side out.

4. Cut the cord in half. Insert a length of cord through the casing on the front; repeat for the back. Thread both ends of the cord on one side through a bead; knot the ends together. Repeat for the cord ends on the other side.

General Instructions

This section includes basic techniques to assist you in creating the projects in this book. Refer to it often if you have questions about specific quilting techniques. It is my goal to keep it simple and direct so that you can enjoy the process and be thrilled with your new look. Begin by reviewing a few important tips:

- Cotton yardages are based on 42"-wide fabrics unless stated otherwise.
- Cut carefully. Use a mat, acrylic ruler, and sharp rotary cutter.
- Consistent seam allowances are a must.
- Chain piecing is a simple, time-saving technique.
- Correct measurements can be achieved by measuring twice and cutting once.
- Carefully press after each step.

Embellishing with Faux Chenille

You can add pizzazz to any project by incorporating Chenille by the Inch into your design. This fun faux chenille is very durable and gets softer and fluffier when it's washed. The fabric has already been layered and stitched for you; all you need to do is cut the fabric into strips. The resulting bias strips are flexible and work beautifully to accent curved shapes. The following are a few simple tips for working with faux chenille strips.

- Mark the pattern designs on the base fabric with a water-soluble pen.
- Remove the tear-away backing from the packaged fabric. Using a rotary cutter and ruler, cut the fabric piece into strips. Center the ruler between the stitching lines.
- Backstitch at the beginning and end of each strip. For a line that is longer than one chenille strip, overlap strips ¼", backstitch, and continue sewing.
- After the strips are stitched in place, lightly spray the strips with water to dampen them; use a chenille brush to loosen the fibers and fluff the chenille.

Making Custom Piping

Give your project a professional touch by inserting coordinating piping between the seams. Ready-made piping is available at fabric shops, but unfortunately it is only available in a limited range of solid colors and an even more limited number of prints. To get perfectly coordinated piping every time, make your own by simply covering a length of cording with the fabric of your choice. You can see how great custom piping looks on "Chenille Duvet Cover" on page 40. Follow these instructions to make it. The fabric yardage, cord diameter, and cord length will be indicated in the project instructions.

1. Refer to "Bias Binding" on page 92 to cut bias strips the width indicated in the project instructions. Join the strips.

2. With the wrong sides together, wrap the bias strip around the cord so that the raw edges are even. Stitch close to the cord with a zipper foot. You will need to stitch just inside this line of stitching when you attach the cording to the project, so don't stitch as close to the cord as you can at this point.

3. Refer to the project instructions to stitch the piping to the project.

Adding Borders

Borders are added to the quilt after the center blocks are assembled. They can be added to the quilt top by using either the straight-cut method or the mitered method. The edges of the outer border can then be scalloped, if desired.

Whether you are adding straight-cut or mitered borders, the cutting instructions for the project will indicate the width to cut the strips. You will need to measure the quilt top as indicated below *before* you cut the strips to the required length. To achieve the required length, you may need to piece strips together first and then cut from the pieced strip. Piece the strips together as shown for straight-cut binding strips (page 91). Take the time to straighten the edges of your quilt top before adding the borders so that your quilt top will lie flat.

Straight-Cut Borders

1. Measure the length of the quilt top through the center. Cut two border strips to this measurement, piecing as necessary. Mark the center of the quilt edges and the border strips. Pin the border strips to the sides of the quilt top, matching the center marks and ends and easing as necessary; stitch. Press the seams toward the border strips.

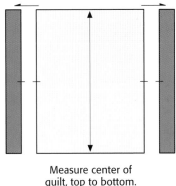

Measure center of
quilt, top to bottom.
Mark centers.

2. Measure the width of the quilt top through the center, including the side border strips just added. Cut two border strips to this measurement, piecing as necessary. Mark the center of the top and bottom edges of the quilt top and the border strips. Pin the border strips to the top and bottom edges of the quilt top, matching the center marks and ends and easing as necessary; stitch. Press the seams toward the border strips.

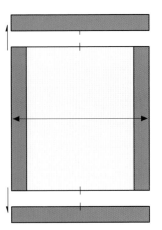

Measure center of quilt,
side to side, including borders.
Mark centers.

Mitered Borders

Strips for mitered borders are cut extra long and trimmed to fit after stitching the mitered corners.

1. Calculate the final outside measurement of the quilt. To do this, measure through the vertical and horizontal centers of the quilt top. Make a note of each measurement. Add twice the width of the border strip plus an additional 2" to 3" to each measurement. Cut two border strips the width indicated in the project instructions and the length calculated for the vertical measurement. Repeat for the horizontal measurement.

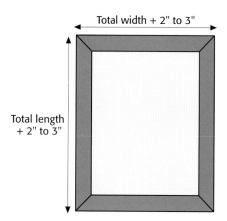

2. Pin-mark the center of each border strip and the center of each quilt edge. On each border strip, also measure and pin-mark one-half the length (or width) of the quilt top (without borders) from each side of the center pin. With right sides together, pin the top border strip to the top edge of the quilt, matching the centers. Also match the outer pins to the ends of the quilt top. An even amount of the excess border strip should extend beyond each end of the quilt top. Stitch, beginning

and ending with a backstitch ¼" from the quilt-top corners. Repeat with the remaining border strips.

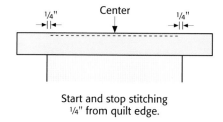

Start and stop stitching ¼" from quilt edge.

3. Lay the quilt top on a flat surface. Working with the border strips at one corner, place one border on top of the other at a 90° angle.

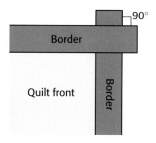

4. Turn the top border layer back at a 45° angle and press to mark the stitching line.

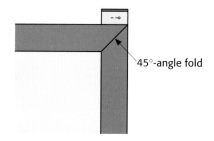

45°-angle fold

5. With right sides together, pin the borders together and sew on the pressed crease, backstitching as you begin and end the stitching.

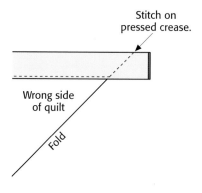

Stitch on pressed crease.

Wrong side of quilt

Fold

6. Trim away the excess border fabric, leaving a ¼" seam allowance. Press the seam open. Repeat with the remaining corners.

Trim mitered seams
and press open.

Scalloped Edges

A scalloped edge can be added to the outermost border once it is attached. To scallop the edge, follow these steps:

1. Cut a piece of freezer paper the width of the side border and the full length of one side of your quilt top. Lay the quilt top on a flat surface; align the freezer paper, shiny side down, with the inner edge of the quilt top; and pencil-mark the mitered corners.

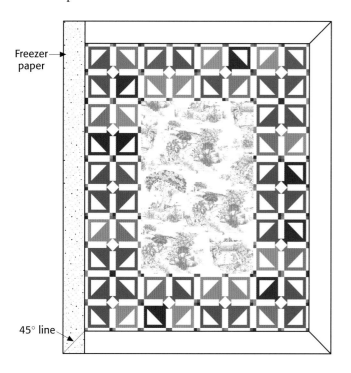

Freezer paper

45° line

2. Mark a straight line on the freezer paper at the desired width of the scalloped edge.

3. Starting with a corner, place a plate or other round object of the desired diameter on the freezer paper and mark around the top portion to make the first scalloped corner. Repeat in the opposite corner of the freezer-paper strip. Working from both ends and moving toward the center, continue to draw arcs along the strip. Adjust the size of the center arc if needed by drawing a larger arc to fit the remaining space. For smaller scallops, overlap the plate tracings and gently round the dips to create a nice flowing effect.

4. Lift the freezer paper off of the quilt top and cut out the scalloped pattern on the marked lines. Place the pattern back on the side of the quilt you removed it from, shiny side down, and lightly iron it in place. Mark the scalloped edge with a water-soluble marker. Carefully peel off the freezer paper, rotate it 180°, and reposition it on the opposite side; mark the scalloped edge.

5. Repeat steps 1–4 for the top and bottom, cutting the freezer-paper strip to fit between the marked sides and continuing the lines from the sides onto the new paper strip. These marked lines help the quilter know exactly how the border will finish and she can quilt accordingly without having to deal with the actual scalloped edges.

> ➤ **Fearless Scalloped Borders** ◄
>
> I knew I wanted a scalloped border on the "Basket Quilt" but writing precise instructions using my usual "dinner plate" method was going to be a challenge. After doing a little shopping, I found several tools designed to assist me in making quick and accurate scallops. In the end, however, I returned to my tried-and-true 10" dinner plate. Check the notions department of your local quilt shop for scalloping tools and follow the manufacturer's instructions, or run to the kitchen and grab a dinner plate. Either way, it's not as hard as it looks.

Layering the Quilt

Quilt shops and some fabric stores sell 90"- and 108"-wide cotton fabric that is very practical for backing quilts. However, the instructions in this book always give backing yardage based on 42"-wide fabric.

When using 42"-wide fabric, all quilts wider than 36" will require a pieced backing. It is necessary to sew two or three lengths of fabric together to make a backing of the required size.

Trim away the selvage edges before sewing the lengths together. Press the backing seams open to make quilting easier.

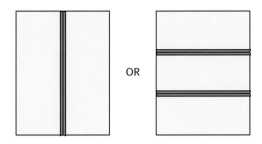

1. Lay the pressed backing on a flat surface, wrong side up. Anchor it with masking tape, being careful not to stretch the fabric out of shape.

2. Spread the batting over the backing, smoothing out any wrinkles.

3. Center the pressed quilt top on the top of the batting with the right side up. Smooth out any wrinkles and make sure the quilt-top edges are parallel to the edges of the backing.

4. Baste with hand stitching or with safety pins.

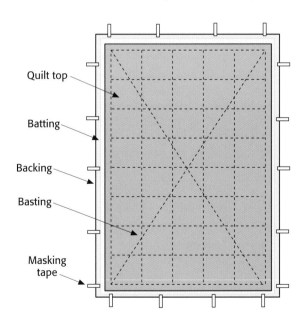

Quilt top

Batting

Backing

Basting

Masking tape

Quilting

Choose your favorite method to quilt your project. All of the projects in this book were machine quilted. There are some excellent books on machine and hand quilting. Check with your favorite quilt shop for current publications. The following are a few guidelines for machine quilting.

◆ Machine quilting is suitable for all quilt types, from wall hangings to full-size bed quilts. With machine quilting, you can quickly complete a quilt that might otherwise remain just a quilt top.

◆ For straight-line quilting, it is extremely helpful to have a walking foot to feed the quilt layers through the machine without shifting or puckering. Some machines have a built-in walking foot or even-feed feature; other machines require a separate attachment.

◆ Use free-motion quilting to outline a quilt pattern in the fabric or to create stippling and many other curved designs. You will need a darning foot and the ability to drop the feed dogs on your machine. Instead of turning the fabric to change directions, you guide the fabric in the direction of the design and use the needle like a pencil.

Adding a Hanging Sleeve

If you plan to display your quilts, and I hope you will, attach a hanging sleeve or rod pocket to the back before attaching the binding.

1. From the leftover backing or quilt-top fabric, cut an 8"-wide strip of fabric long enough to equal the width of your quilt. You may need to piece several different strips together for larger quilts. On each end, fold under ½",

and then fold ½" again. Press and stitch by machine.

½" ½"

2. Fold the strip in half lengthwise, wrong sides together; baste the raw edges to the top edge on the back of your quilt. These will be enclosed when you sew on the binding. Your quilt should be about 1" wider than the sleeve on both ends. Allow a little slack in the sleeve to accommodate the rod thickness; slipstitch the ends and bottom edge of the sleeve to the backing.

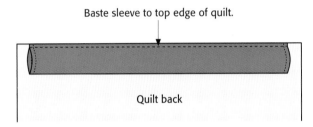

Baste sleeve to top edge of quilt.

Quilt back

Binding

If your quilt has curved edges, you must bind your quilt with bias-cut strips so that the binding curves smoothly around the edges. For straight edges, use the straight-cut binding technique.

Straight-Cut Binding

For a French double-fold binding, cut strips as instructed in the project. Binding strips cut 2½" wide will result in a finished binding that is about ½" wide.

1. With right sides together, sew the binding strips together on the diagonal as shown to create one long strip. Trim the excess fabric and press the seams open.

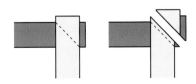

2. Cut one end of the strip at a 45° angle and press it under ¼". Press the strip in half lengthwise, wrong sides together.

Fold line

3. Beginning on one side of the quilt and using a ¼" seam allowance, stitch the binding to the quilt. Keep the raw edges even with the edge of the quilt top. Use a walking foot, if you have one, to feed the layers through the machine evenly. Stop stitching ¼" from the corner of the quilt and backstitch. Clip the thread.

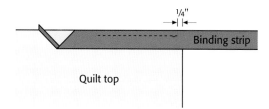

¼"

Binding strip

Quilt top

4. Turn the quilt so that you will be stitching down the next side. Fold the binding up, away from the quilt and then back down onto itself, keeping the raw edges even. Begin stitching at the edge, backstitch, and continue to the next corner, stopping ¼" from the end. Repeat the process for the corners and remaining sides.

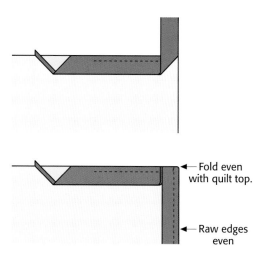

Fold even with quilt top.

Raw edges even

5. When you reach the starting point, lap the strip over the beginning stitches by about 1" and cut away any excess binding, trimming the end at a 45° angle. Tuck the end of the binding into the fold and complete the seam.

6. Fold the binding over the raw edges to the back, covering the row of machine stitching. Slipstitch the binding in place, mitering the corners.

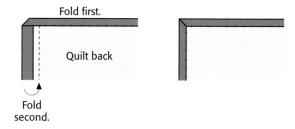

Fold first.

Quilt back

Fold second.

Bias Binding

Stripes or plaids look especially dramatic when they are cut on the bias and used for bindings.

1. Place a single layer of fabric on a rotary-cutting mat. Using a ruler with a 45°-angle marking, align the 45°-angle line with an edge of the fabric as shown. Cut as many strips as needed to achieve the required length in the width indicated for the project.

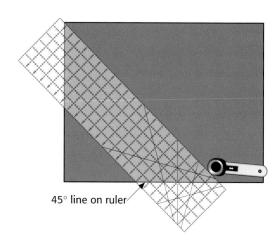

45° line on ruler

2. With right sides together, sew the strips together, offsetting the seams by ¼" as shown. Stitch and press the seams open.

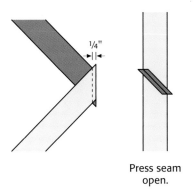

Press seam
open.

3. Follow steps 2–6 of "Straight-Cut Binding" on page 91 to stitch the binding to the quilt edges.

Attaching a Label

It is a good plan to label a quilt with its name, the maker, and the year it was made. I used to feel that my quilts weren't special enough to label, but regrettably I have already forgotten some of the fun details of my earlier efforts. Since then I have discovered a computer program that allows me to easily print my own unique labels on cotton fabric and I get quite zealous about this detail. Of course, you can use a permanent-ink pen and plain cotton to make a simple label that accomplishes the same purpose.

These days I am printing story labels for my antique quilts, giving any information that I can glean, including how I acquired the quilt, its approximate age, and block names. Now when the quilts are handed off, the next recipient doesn't have to search for information about the quilt and doesn't have to be a quilter to know its interesting details.

Suggested Reading List

Part of what makes another good quilt book possible is building on the ideas and successes of others. The following are just a few of my favorites that I think you, too, will find helpful and inspirational.

Martin, Nancy J. *Beyond the Blocks*. Woodinville, WA.: Martingale & Company, 2002.

Mostek, Pamela. *Just Can't Cut It!* Woodinville, WA.: Martingale & Company, 2003.

Mostek, Pamela, and Jean Van Bockel. *Quilts from Larkspur Farm*. Woodinville, WA.: Martingale & Company, 2002.

Triangle Tricks. Woodinville, WA.: Martingale & Company, 2003.

About the Author

Re-creating the charm of yesterday's retro look by using today's quick quilting techniques and tools is a specialty of Patti's. For inspiration, she uses her memories of colorful childhood quilts and combines them with another vintage favorite, chenille, to create the quilts and other home-decorating projects in this, her first solo book.

But the vintage look isn't Patti's only love. Her creative career includes years of watercolor painting, sewing, and quilting. Today she owns a quilt shop and divides her time between it; her pattern company, Hawthorne Handworks; and a variety of other creative passions, from flower arranging to painting decorative furniture.

Patti grew up on a farm in rural Washington State, and she has resided there most of her life. She also manages to squeeze in time to be a wife, a mother, and a grandmother.